Michael Doe became General Secretary of the Anglican mission agency, USPG: Anglicans in World Mission, in 2004. He has been Youth Secretary of the British Council of Churches, a parish priest on housing estates in London and Oxford, and Social Responsibility Officer in the Diocese of Portsmouth. In 1994 he became the first Bishop of Swindon, and is now an Assistant Bishop in the Diocese of Southwark.

SAVING POWER

SAVING POWER

The Anglican Communion and the Mission of God

Michael Doe

First published in Great Britain in 2011

Society for Promoting Christian Knowledge
36 Causton Street
London SW1P 4ST
www.spckpublishing.co.uk

British Library Cataloguing-in-Publication Data
A catalogue record for this book is available from the British Library

ISBN 978–0–281–06454–0

1 3 5 7 9 10 8 6 4 2

Typeset by Graphicraft Ltd, Hong Kong
Manufacture managed by Jellyfish
Printed in Great Britain by CPI

Produced on paper from sustainable forests

Contents

———•◆•———

Contents

Introduction

Does mission matter? For a lot of British people mission is what the missionaries did during the time of the Empire, or what we need to do today to 'sell' the Church in our kind of consumerist society. Does the worldwide Church matter, or more particularly that part of it which has become the Anglican Communion? Again, for many people in the North it's either a leftover from the days of Empire or an increasingly irritating place where conservatives and liberals argue over what most people here see as secondary issues. I want to say that mission is the lifeblood of the Church, and our understanding of it is crucial not only for how we belong together in the Anglican Communion but also for what we present to the wider world. My starting point is a deep loyalty to the Anglican way of being Church, but an even deeper commitment to God's mission – the *Missio Dei* – in the world.

An underlying theme of this book is power. How has power been exercised in God's Church, especially during the colonial period, and how should it be used in the Anglican Communion today? And how does that relate to how we understand power in the Mission of God, and especially in what we see in Jesus Christ?

The Society for the Propagation of the Gospel, whose successor (USPG) I now serve as General Secretary, played an important part in the outreach of the Church of England across the world. The story of how the Church of England spawned the Anglican Communion touches on a number of issues, many of which continue to underlie our life today and the problems we face. Historically there are the military and political events, and the economic needs and opportunities, that create and sustain empires; the starting point of this book must be the British Empire, which by 1921 ruled over a quarter of the world's population, and then the US empire which has succeeded it. Sociologically and culturally there are the issues relating to colonialism, concerning the values and institutions (including Christianity and the Church) that were exported to these other peoples, what that did to them, and the resulting relationships. Of particular importance here, in seeking to understand the contemporary Anglican Communion, is what happened when the Empire was dissolved and in what sense we are now post-colonial. Then, theologically, although inevitably linked to other cultural values and to the role of the institutional Church, there is the need to define, first, the nature of mission, what it meant then and what it means now, and, second, what is distinctive within this from the Anglican tradition.

As I've said, underlying all of this is the theme of power, its use during colonial and post-colonial days, the part it plays in the current conflicts of the Anglican Communion, and what the Christian tradition has to say about it as part of mission and in how the Church is run. And throughout all this discussion of colonialism and post-colonialism, and of what we mean by mission, tradition and communion itself, there are the questions raised by what some call post-modernism, which are about definitions and who decides them – a subject, again, very closely linked to issues of power. That takes us into the worlds of post-imperialism: how old empires have given way to new ones within the process of globalization, and how this also impacts on the Church; and of post-colonialism: how colonial patterns and powers determined communion and mission, and where the post-colonial future lies.

Faced with such large and challenging matters, and with all the resulting conflicts which today seem to dominate the Anglican Communion, one might be tempted to withdraw into one's own local church and forget the wider world, were it not for the fact that globalization is now something from which none of us can escape. Equally tempting are the two ways in which much of the world makes its response, either by retreating into what are deemed past certainties or by embracing a consumer culture which talks of freedom and choice but often imposes new forms of domination. Both of these can be seen in the way that Anglicans are responding to the Communion's present problems. I believe that there are better ways forward in which, ironic though it may seem with our current conflicts, the Anglican Communion has an essential contribution to make. This comes from out of our history and today's struggles, from a rediscovery of the Anglican Way, and most of all from the God in whose global, indeed cosmic mission we seek to share.

It will be helpful to define some terms at the outset. In general I prefer to allow people to label themselves, while aware that in the continuum from conservativism to liberalism, the claims at one end to be 'traditionalist' and at the other to be 'inclusivist' may be strongly contested by the other side.

The words 'North' and 'South' (or alternatively, 'The West') are a useful shorthand but can hide other differences. Much post-colonial thinking has talked more about 'Westernization' and 'Orientalism'. In looking at the Anglican Communion a useful definition of 'the South' is those Provinces who associated themselves with the 'Global South' movement in the 1990s (see Chapter 2), most of whom officially attended the Global Anglican Future Conference (GAFCON) event in 2008. However, there are many churches in the southern hemisphere which are not part of this movement – most significantly those in southern Africa, Brazil, Australia (apart from Sydney) and New Zealand – and many in Asia and the Pacific who are at best ambivalent towards it.

I tend to use the word 'America', rightly or wrongly, for the United States, or 'North America' when it includes Canada. Finally, I refer to the Anglican Church in the United States as 'The Episcopal Church' or 'TEC', the name it has generally preferred to use since 1979 (although its legal name remains the Domestic and Foreign Missionary Society of the Protestant Episcopal Church in the USA, reflecting its belief, held since 1821, that mission is the responsibility of every church member rather than of some separate mission agency).

In the chapters that follow I begin by exploring how the Anglican Communion came into being (Chapters 1 and 2) and what has led to its present problems (Chapter 3). I then turn to examine how we understand mission (Chapter 4) and how this finds expression in the Communion today (Chapter 5). The following chapter attempts some analysis from the perspectives of post-modernism, post-colonialism and globalization. A final chapter looks to the future of both mission and Communion.

1

The expansion of the Church of England

The Church of England

The story of the Church of England is only one part of the history of the Christian Church,[1] and the Church of England today is a relatively small section of what is now called world Christianity.[2] But the Church of England has played a large part in forming the English nation and character, and was the starting point of what is now the worldwide Anglican Communion.

The *ecclesia Anglicana* did not begin at the Reformation, and those responsible for the changes that happened in that period were keen to establish its continuity with what had gone before and indeed to defend what they did as a return to the principles of the early Church. Exactly when Christianity arrived on the shores of Britain is unknown. Maybe it came with the Phoenician traders with whom are associated the Glastonbury legends of Joseph of Arimathea and the Holy Grail, and the even less plausible story that on a first visit he brought the child Jesus with him. Certainly it was here by the time the Roman Empire extended as far as Hadrian's Wall, an era during which St Alban is said to have been the first English martyr. Other Christian pioneers had already established a more 'Celtic' Christianity in Ireland, from which further missionary work established churches in the north and west of the British mainland.

In 597 new missionaries came from Rome. The story goes that the man who later became Pope Gregory was in the marketplace in Rome, where among the slaves on display were a couple of striking children with blond hair and blue eyes. On asking their origins he was told they were Angles. He declared that these Angles looked like angels, and that it was therefore time their people were converted to Christianity. On the basis of what one English humorist has called a very weak pun,[3] Gregory sent his reluctant emissary Augustine to begin the work, with the instruction that Augustine 'should by no means destroy the temples of the gods but rather the idols within those temples . . . thus, if [the people] are not deprived of all the exterior joys they will more easily taste the interior ones'. He clearly understood the relationship between mission and inculturation!

St Augustine's mission meant that there were now two Christian traditions in England – one looking to Rome, the other more at home in the Celtic lands where the Roman Empire had made less impact. A century later these two 'churches of England' got together at the Synod of Whitby, and by the end the Celtic Church had given way to the Roman one. Like many Synods since, they talked a lot about truth, but in the end power won – in this case, the power of the Pope.

England was now clearly part of European Christendom, but tensions between what may be called the imperial and the national were never far below the surface. Before his invasion in 1066 William the Conqueror sought and obtained the support of Pope Alexander II, but then refused to pay fealty to his successor. In 1170 Thomas Becket lost his life defending the rights of the Pope, but the king was forced to do public penance to recover the loyalty of the faithful.

Such tensions came to a head at the beginning of the sixteenth century when Renaissance thinking, the rise of Continental Protestantism, increasing nationalism at home, and the needs of Henry VIII both for an heir and to satisfy his own libido, all came together in the English Reformation. Making use of a title which had been given him by the Pope in happier times, the king presented himself as the 'Defender of the Faith' who was cleansing the Church of corruption, although recent scholarship has questioned how far it warranted such attention.[4]

Imperial expansion

This was also the time of European expansionism, as Catholic Spain, Portugal and then France claimed empires and boasted that they were extending Christendom. As the conquistadores took control of Latin America they exchanged goods (including enslaved people) for European civilization and its religion. In America today, 12 October is Columbus Day, a national holiday, but some prefer to celebrate it as Survivors' Day, remembering those who were living in places where whole peoples and cultures were devastated by European guns and disease.

In all these empires the invaders and traders were soon followed by the Church. Those sent to Christianize the colonized territories were called 'missionaries', and their assignment was called 'mission', terms first used by Ignatius of Loyola. A series of fifteenth-century papal bulls led to the Doctrine of Discovery, an essentially racist philosophy that legitimized the claims of the white Christian Europeans.[5] In 1494 Pope Alexander VI divided up the New World between Spain and Portugal. He was also defending his own imperial interests: as late as 1940, the Vatican signed an 'Acordo Missionario' with Portugal, allying colonial and church power in the Portuguese empire.

A century later Protestant Holland and England were also in the game. The first Anglican services in North America were held when Martin Frobisher landed in Canada in 1578 (England was still Roman Catholic when John Cabot was there in 1497), and by Sir Francis Drake in California a year later. In 1606 James I signed a charter for the Virginia Company which included the 'propagating of Christian Religion to such people as yet live in darkness and miserable ignorance of the true knowledge and worship of God and may in time bring the infidels and savages living in these parts to human civility and to a settled and quiet government'.[6]

In 1649, the year that King Charles I was beheaded, the Commonwealth Parliament in Westminster gave a charter to found a missionary organization called the Society for the Propagation of the Gospel in New England with the purpose of converting New England Indians. By the time the monarchy was restored, the overseas development of the Church of England was already challenging the insular view of the Church at home. The 1662 Book of Common Prayer had to address the spiritual concerns of the contemporary adventurer. It notes in the Preface that:

it was thought convenient, that some Prayers and Thanksgivings, fitted to special occasions, should be added in their due places; particularly for those at Sea, together with an office for the Baptism of such as are of Riper Years: which, although not so necessary when the former Book was compiled, . . . is now become necessary, and may be always useful for the baptizing of Natives in our Plantations, and others converted to the Faith.

The Bishop of London's jurisdiction now included 'English congregations gathering abroad and the clergy ministering to them', and in 1685 he appointed Commissaries to oversee this work. The first of these, Thomas Bray, visited Maryland in 1699. Bray had already established the Society for the Promotion of Christian Knowledge (SPCK) and in 1701 he secured a Royal Charter for a new organization, the Society for the Propagation of the Gospel in Foreign Parts (SPG), to meet the needs of the Church in North America.[7] Bray's primary aim was to confront the 'superstitious blasphemies, heresies and fooleries' of 'Papists, Dissenters . . . and Quakers', but having started with 'our own people' the Society soon moved on to the natives, 'who may by this be converted from that state of barbarism and idolatry in which they now live'.[8] By 1710 its London Committee was saying that 'The design of propagating the Gospel in foreign parts chiefly concerns the conversion of the heathen, and this must be placed first'.[9]

SPG sent missionaries and funds to support the established Church. It was, says William Jacob, 'as near as the circumstances of the time would permit an official body of the C of E'.[10] The Archbishop of Canterbury, or in his absence the Bishop of London, chaired its monthly meetings. Income came from private subscriptions and collections in each parish which were authorized by royal command.[11] By the time of the American War of Independence the Society had sent 600 missionaries across the Atlantic.

This presence of the Church of England was opposed by the Congregationalists in New England, and by other colonial settlers who wanted to distance themselves from the British monarch: it was these people, rather than the Church of England itself, who were the main reason why no bishop was appointed, with the result that everyone who wanted to be ordained had to sail to London. Many of the colonists also resisted the Society's outreach to slaves via such groups as the

Catechizing School in New York, and its work among the native peoples which was particularly successful among the Mohawk Indians.

SPG was limited by its charter to ministering to English settlers in the colonies and to native people subject to the British crown, so when the Americans severed links with the English monarch, and by implication with the established Church, the Society turned its attention north and south. It already had missionaries in Nova Scotia, and the Church began to spread through the rest of Canada. Charles Inglis became the first bishop in 1787 and by 1900 there were 16 dioceses across the country.

To the south, the Church of England had taken root in the West Indies, especially in Barbados, but it is here that one of the most shameful episodes in its history took place. In 1710 Governor-General Christopher Codrington left his sugar cane estates to SPG so that it could establish a quasi-monastic missionary college. He also bequeathed the 300 slaves needed to work the estates. Although the bishops running the Society in London took some interest in the welfare of the slaves, including their instruction and conversion, it was a different matter on the ground: the slaves were branded and often ill-treated. Noel Titus, Principal of what became the seminary at Codrington, condemns the Society for its failure to agitate against the slave trade.[12] Emancipation finally came in 1834, and the Church of England continued to grow around the Caribbean. Bishops were appointed for Barbados and Jamaica in 1824, but it was only in 1951 that a West Indian was elected.

The other corner of the transatlantic slave triangle was West Africa. Anglican missionary activity began here in 1752 when SPG sent Thomas Thompson to be chaplain to the fort at Cape Coast (in what is now Ghana) and to its government-funded slaving station. Thompson was an ardent defender of the slave trade but also wanted to promote Christianity among Africans, which is why he found a young African convert called Philip Quaque and sent him to London. After seven years Quaque was ordained as the first non-European priest in the Church of England and in 1765 returned home, but he was alienated both from his fellow-Africans, whom he sought to educate, and from the English supervisors of the slave trade who generally ignored or even ridiculed his ministry.

Meanwhile, the British Empire was growing in other parts of the world, with the Church of England not far behind. In some parts of Africa the missionaries preceded those with more material interests, in others the Church was seen as an essential ally: according to William Knox, Under-Secretary of State for the Colonies in 1786, 'The Prevalence of the Church of England in these colonies is the best security that Great Britain can have for their Fidelity and attachment to her Constitutions and Interests.'[13]

At this stage Britain's main concern was to generate trade so as to improve the lot of people back home rather than to govern foreign countries or improve their peoples. This was especially true in India, where the East India Company accepted Anglican and Lutheran chaplains to minister to Europeans but held out until 1813 against missionaries through suspicion that they would create unrest and damage trade. The story is still told in Chennai (Madras) that the Company asked SPG if the Magnificat could be omitted in Evensong lest 'putting down the mighty' might inflame the natives.[14] The stability of the Empire was paramount, and there was fear of anything which would make it impossible for thirty thousand 'white men' to govern seventy million 'sable subjects' across the world.

Thomas Thomason, an East India Company chaplain, in 1814 bemoaned their state: 'We have annihilated the political importance of the natives, stripped them of their power, and laid them prostrate, without giving them anything in return.'[15] Others questioned whether the British Empire had any mandate to overturn the religion of another country. Back in Britain the cleric and satirist Sydney Smith was among those who attacked the missionaries in India as 'little detachments of maniacs', considering that 'The rapid or speedy conversion of the whole world to Christianity forms no part of the schemes of its Almighty Governor.' Priority, he said, must be to 'our duties to our families, to our neighbours, and to our country [as] set before us by God himself'.[16]

Revivalism in the Church

The Church of England did not greatly flourish in the eighteenth century. In 1747 Joseph Butler, distinguished scholar and Bishop of Bristol, is reputed to have declined appointment as Archbishop of Canterbury on the grounds that it was 'too late to support a falling Church'.[17]

Towards the end of the century the church in England began to experience an evangelical revival. The founders of Methodism, John and Charles Wesley, having returned from missionary work in North America with SPG, first laboured for it within the Church of England. In 1792 William Carey, who went on to found the Baptist Missionary Society, published a tract declaring – as Thomas Bray had done before him – that the Great Commission of Jesus[18] to go out into all the world still held. And in 1799 a group of activist evangelical clergymen, supported by the Clapham Sect and including William Wilberforce, created what was to become the Church Missionary Society.

The founders of CMS were committed to three great enterprises: abolition of the slave trade, social reform at home and world evangelization. When Church of England clergy failed to come forward for overseas service in the expected numbers, CMS turned towards the Lutherans. German pietists, especially Moravians, had often pioneered such work. CMS's overseas mission began in Sierra Leone in 1804 but spread rapidly to India, Canada and the area around the Mediterranean.

Compared to the new zeal which CMS brought to the missionary enterprise, SPG at this time has been characterized as a somewhat subservient chaplaincy to the established Church around the Empire, but this is not the whole story. For example, in his 1773 anniversary sermon for the Society, Bishop Shipley of St Asaph said:

> It ought not to be the first object of contemplation, what we are to get by them [i.e. colonies]; but how we can best improve, assist and reward them; by what benefits we may procure their happiness and win their affection.... And let us endeavour to wipe away the tears from the poor oppressed natives of India; and suffer them, if possible, to enjoy some taste of the legal security and civil liberty, which renders life dear to ourselves; which are blessings hitherto unknown to those climates.[19]

Early in the nineteenth century SPG was itself revitalized by the Hackney Phalanx, a group of High Church clergy and laymen who saw the Church of England as a branch of the Universal Church, sealed by apostolic succession. Some years later the Oxford Movement breathed new life into the missionary efforts of SPG, but even more into a new mission agency – the Universities Mission to Central Africa (UMCA). In1965 it merged with SPG to create the United Society for the Propagation of the Gospel (USPG). Founded in response to a call from the explorer David Livingstone to take 'commerce and Christianity' to Africa, which he believed was the only way to combat the slave trade, it was responsible for creating in what is now Zambia, Malawi, Mozambique, Botswana and parts of Tanzania a church which still treasures its Anglo-Catholic origins.

The first UMCA missionary expedition was led by Charles Mackenzie. He and Coleridge Patterson in Melanesia were the first bishops appointed for missionary work outside British jurisdiction. His 1860 mission via the Zambezi was not a success: led astray by what William Jacob calls Livingstone's inaccurate geography and romanticized notions,[20] Mackenzie died within a year, together with four other Europeans and three Africans in his party. It was left to a second UMCA foray in 1864, this time through Zanzibar, for the Church to become established.

And so the Church of England spread around the British Empire. In October 1786, the Revd Richard Johnson received a royal warrant as Chaplain to the Colony of New South Wales and sailed on the first convict ship to Botany Bay, carrying Bibles and Christian books provided by SPG and SPCK. CMS began operations in Sydney in 1825, with the intention of bringing the gospel to the aboriginal population. In 1814 Thomas Middleton was consecrated Bishop of Calcutta, with a diocese covering all the territories of the East India Company. On Christmas Day that year the Revd Samuel Marsden, sent by CMS, performed the first full Christian service in New Zealand. In other places around the world, such as Burma (which became the Province of Myanmar in 1970), the English Church began to attract native peoples. Missionary work in Ceylon, now Sri Lanka, began in 1818. Anglican missionaries began arriving in China in 1834. In Malaysia, now part of the Province of South East Asia, an SPG missionary in Kuching, Francis Thomas McDougal, became the first bishop in 1856. SPG sent Charles J. Corfe to become the first Bishop of Korea in 1889.

In Africa, CMS was largely responsible for what are now the Anglican churches in Uganda, Kenya, Congo, Rwanda and Burundi, teaching a kind of theology and ecclesiology – later reinforced by the East African evangelical revival – which may explain something about why those Provinces have identified themselves with one particular side of the Anglican Communion's current division.

Unlike SPG, CMS always saw itself as a voluntary society, but its leaders also believed that Establishment through Parliament helped protect the Church from the doctrines and more monarchical style of Catholic-minded bishops. For the same reason they resisted the appointment of bishops outside the Queen's dominions, and questioned the validity of bishops in a church, like the American one, which was not so established. They generally preferred to see bishops appointed after the Church had been established, and in the early nineteenth century in both Jamaica and Calcutta they resisted the authority of the local bishop to control their missionaries. They also felt their independence threatened by George Selwyn, whose appointment as the 'missionary bishop' to New Zealand combined both missionary and colonial roles.

Later, other mission agencies came into being, such as the South American Missionary Society (now part of CMS) for work in Spanish-speaking Latin America. In 1922 the Bible Churchman's Mission Society (now Crosslinks) split from CMS following a doctrinal dispute between liberal and conservative evangelicals. Among the increasing number of missionaries women played a large part: from the 1890s they were in the majority, reinforcing the 'welfare' aspects of mission.[21]

The new imperialism

It was comparatively late in its history that the British Empire reached what is now seen as its full imperial glory, but towards the end of the nineteenth century this 'new imperialism' was gaining strength. The 1885 Berlin Conference, called by Bismarck to settle the carving-up of Africa by the European powers, led more nations, including Germany and Italy, to seek land and control overseas. The European empires are said to have held sway over more than 85 per cent of the rest of the globe by the time of the First World War. They sought justification for this, together with the right to destroy other cultures and make use of their wealth, in the theory of social Darwinism[22] and the consequent belief in the superiority of European civilization.

For Britain a dual mandate to benefit domestic industry and improve 'native races' abroad became more pronounced. Echoing David Livingstone, the belief grew that civilization and commerce belonged with conversion. So in 1882 Sir John Seeley, in his *The Expansion of England*, was happy to defend this Anglo-Saxon vocation to dominate the world, and Bishop Barry's 1894–95 Hulsean Lectures were entitled 'The Ecclesiastical Expansion of England'. Where the missionary enterprise failed, especially when confronting Islam, evangelicalism became more individualistic and other-worldly. It also became increasingly millennial, which may be seen as another form of imperialism, believing that God will soon intervene to take over the world and reinstate those whose rightful position has not been given its due recognition.

Many in the missionary movements embraced this imperial expansion, and some likened it to the providential existence of the Roman Empire which allowed the early Church to permeate the then known world. In 1907 the President of CMS wrote of their missionary in the Sudan:

> [Mr Lloyd] has been bearing his share of 'the white man's burden' of ruling, civilizing and Christianizing the 'silent peoples' of whom John Bull carries no less than 350 millions on his back. . . . The duty is no light one, but it gives an outlet for the energies of our people, an object worthy of an Imperial race, of a Christian country, a call to put forth the highest qualities of the Anglo-Saxon character.[23]

Others, like George Lefroy, who went out to join the Delhi Brotherhood and became Bishop of Lahore and then Calcutta, felt more compromised, saying in 1880: 'I believe that our position as the ruling power puts a dead weight on the missionary enterprise which nothing but the direct grace of God can possibly enable us to lift.'[24] In 1907, Roland Allen, who had served as an SPG missionary in China from 1895 to 1903, resigned from the Society, denouncing the imperial structures of the whole missionary enterprise. Missionaries, he said, should be more like St Paul, giving leadership and control to new believers from the outset, and relying on the Holy Spirit rather than external hierarchies.

CMS and SPG benefited from this new imperial enthusiasm but also fell foul of its values. For example, CMS was responsible for the Church in what is now Nigeria, and Henry Venn, the society's notable Secretary from 1841 to 1873, saw it as a prime opportunity to realize his vision for 'the raising up of a Native Church – self-supporting, self-governing, self-extending. The Mission is the scaffolding; the Native Church is the edifice.'[25] He talked of churches being built up from local roots and bishops (ideally natives) as the 'crown of the church'.[26]

In 1864 Venn had Samuel Crowther, a freed slave from the Yoruba people, consecrated as the first African Anglican bishop, to serve in the Niger region.[27] Crowther was a product of empire: 'I know my place as a Negro, but I have ever paid my respects to Europeans as the race of our benefactors.'[28] Even so, the increasing flow of young English missionaries, resulting from a growing individualistic evangelicalism at home, refused to accept him. They reflected a general move in the Empire towards a 'trustee' model of European leaders ensuring orthodoxy and good governance.[29] When Crowther died in 1881 the ideas of a self-governing church and the indigenization of the episcopate were abandoned.

Later on an equally disturbing story can be found in SPG, concerning Bishop Montgomery, its Secretary from 1902 to 1918, who believed that 'These are great times and one feels the stir of an Imperial Christianity.'[30] Sailing to Britain from his former post as Bishop of Tasmania, he wrote that 'clergy are officers in an imperial army', and that when 'full of the Imperial spirit, not merely of the empire of England but of something still greater, the empire of Christ', they could overcome both the sectarianism within the Church of England and the lack of zeal which was impeding missionary advance around the world.[31] Anglicanism, he believed, could include many races but only if the Church of England assumed its proper vocation to lead them: his imperialism was an 'explicit geo-religious jingoism linked to an explicit if self-contradictory evocation of racial hierarchies'.[32]

Mission and imperialism

Desmond Tutu is wont to tell this parable, first heard among the Xhosa people in his native South Africa. 'When the white man first came here, he had the Bible and we had the land. The white man said to us, "Come, let us kneel and pray together." So we knelt and prayed, and when we opened our eyes again, lo! – we had the Bible and he had the land.' He tells it with that characteristic chuckle which may draw the sting but does not hide the truth.

How far did the missionaries serve the Empire and how far did they serve the gospel? The fact is that few of them would have understood such a 'post-colonial' question, but here are five different assessments.

Brian Stanley criticizes the missionaries for identifying the gospel with civilization as represented by the Enlightenment-driven, industrialized West – the religion of the Victorian middle classes – but also sees them as humanitarians because they did not relegate the gospel to the religious sphere, as much Enlightenment thinking wanted, and unlike much (often racist) post-Enlightenment scientific thinking they believed in the advance and potential of all people. And, ironically, it was often the more conservative missionaries who were the more suspicious of the claims of Western civilization.[33]

Stephen Neill gives the missionaries credit for defending indigenous people, although not always wisely or indeed with much empathy, and for supporting colonial power as the better protection for converts and oppressed people. On the other hand they welcomed colonial expansion out of a belief that the spread of Western culture and evangelism belonged together, and they usually thought that they were a better judge of the common good than the local people.[34]

John H. Darch calls them 'incidental imperialists':

> although there were a few dedicated imperialists in the missionary ranks . . . the majority had no such enthusiasm. Yet this did not mean that they had no effect on imperial development. By their very presence [and] as providers of education and European moral and spiritual values, missionaries became incidental and sometimes unintentional but nevertheless effective agents of imperialism.[35]

Yet over time, according to Norman Etherington, they also had the opposite effect. Their work in translation, education and health brought Western ideas of individualism, opportunities for women, democracy, science, all of which added to other modernizing changes. Although they may have been reluctant to hand over power to local leadership or to welcome nationalistic movements when the time came, in many ways they had prepared the ground: 'Missionaries, who aimed to replace indigenous cultures with European "civilization" and who frequently allied themselves with colonial governments, nevertheless transmitted a religion which subjugated peoples turned to their own purposes: spiritual, economic, and political.'[36]

Around the Anglican Communion today it is more usual to hear positive than negative responses to the missionary inheritance. Indeed, Lamin Sanneh, an African who is now Professor of Missions at Yale, accuses Western scholars of cultural relativism in many of their critical assessments. He argues – contrary to what he says passes for social science, and in sharp contrast to Islam – that Christianity preserved indigenous life and culture, thanks to its emphasis on mother-tongue translation. Where indigenous culture was strong it absorbed Christian life and worship, thereby sustaining and even increasing its vitality.[37]

2

The emergence of the Anglican Communion

———•◦•———

The Church in the USA

So far we have looked at the colonial era mainly from the viewpoint of the British Empire. Europeans often think that the Episcopal Church in the United States did not become a significant player on the Anglican world stage until recent times, or that the USA's own imperial ambitions did not come to the fore until the middle of the twentieth century. Both are untrue, and like the British experience the actual history needs to be examined in order to understand the Anglican Communion today.[1]

After the War of Independence the Episcopal Church found itself with an identity problem. How should it continue in this new nation with its different churches and a Constitution which declared the separation of church and state? One answer was to secure its own bishop, which it did through the Episcopal Church in Scotland: Samuel Seabury was consecrated Bishop of Connecticut in 1784. A General Convention met for the first time the next year, and in 1789 representatives from nine dioceses gathered in Philadelphia to ratify a constitution for the Protestant Episcopal Church in the United States of America.

The 1835 General Convention (led by the high church Bishop Doane of New Jersey) began to look outwards. It elected two missionary bishops for work in the West of the country, and it decided that responsibility for mission should belong to the church itself and not be given to some voluntary society. Soon missionaries were being sent to Greece and to Liberia, the new African state for freed slaves from America.

China followed, and then Japan where an American, Channing Moore Williams, was elected the first bishop in 1866. Work which had begun in Brazil and Cuba was expanded after the creation of a US branch of CMS in 1859.

The colonialism which characterized the European mission era was also in evidence here. First, from the 1840s onwards, the USA had a sense of being 'an elect nation', now sent by God to extend its blessings to the rest of the world. By the end of the century and the Spanish-American War, President McKinley was able to justify the US annexation of the Philippines as necessary to 'civilize and Christianize' them. In 1901 US bishops were appointed for both the Philippines and Puerto Rico.

Second, there developed the 'National Church Ideal', the sense that the Episcopal Church had a unique mission due to its combination of Protestantism and Catholicism, and its commitment to US freedom and democracy. It was a 'chosen people among an elect nation'. Even when its growing emphasis on the social gospel came into conflict with evangelicals and pre-millennialists, all sides maintained the link between evangelization and civilization; 'all agreed that the West had a divine right to conquer the peoples of the world and define reality for them'.[2]

Less unsettled by the First World War than its European counterparts, the Episcopal Church, with its National Church Ideal strengthened by the victory of democracy, carried on exporting around the world its schools, hospitals, and the kind of church characterized by right-ordered sacramental worship. And after the Second World War, the blossoming of civic religion at home gave it renewed confidence in its contribution to worldwide bodies including the Anglican Communion. By the mid-1950s two-thirds of all missionaries around the world were from one of the churches in the USA.

The Communion's first executive officer, Bishop Stephen Bayne, questioned these missiological imperatives of his own church, its association with spreading the American way of life, and the difficulties which came from missionary bishops still owing their accountability and funding to the USA. It was only in the 1960s, with the failures of Vietnam and anti-establishment protests at home, that the church really began to take on board the issues which colonialism raises for mission.

Although the churches in Brazil and the Philippines were given autonomy, the status of places like Puerto Rico and Taiwan, once 'overseas jurisdictions of the Episcopal Church', has not changed much simply because the words 'United States of America' have been removed from the Episcopal Church's title. The aim was to remove the colonial connotation, but it can actually give the opposite impression by sounding rather definitive and possessive to Anglicans in other parts of the Communion!

There is still much to be done by the Episcopal Church to achieve a more mutual and shared basis for mission with other parts of the Communion. Being a channel for international development aid from the US government has not helped. The numbers of missionaries has declined – in contrast to US evangelical churches, where they continue to grow – but people still talk of 'taking the gospel to Africa' or even themselves 'going on mission' for some short-term project. The emphasis is still very much on charity, appealing for money for struggling churches overseas. It is not unknown for African or Latin American dioceses to receive over 90 per cent of their income from the USA, a situation which, as we shall see, becomes all the more problematic if finance becomes dependent on what side the donors have taken in the current disputes.

From colonies to Communion

We return to the story of the Anglican Communion. During the second half of the nineteenth century the 'old Commonwealth' became more independent of Britain, and the Church of England followed suit. Through the 1860s, some bishops in the colonies became 'metropolitans', presiding over other bishops, and some ceased to be under the authority of the Church of England. Self-governing churches began to emerge in South Africa, Canada, Australia and New Zealand, electing their own bishops and, beginning in Australia, developing a more synodical form of church government. They were autonomous but remained members of a wider Communion through their continuing relationship with the Archbishop of Canterbury.

The status of the church in the USA was less clear. When SPG celebrated its 150th anniversary in 1852 Archbishop Sumner sent an invitation to its bishops 'to manifest the essential unity of the Sister Churches of America and England'.[3] For the first time bishops from the USA, the (Episcopal) Church of Scotland and the Church of England (or rather the United Church of England and Ireland) processed together in Westminster Abbey. Colin Podmore records how, while this may have gladdened the hearts of SPG's more high-church leaders, it was not so acceptable to evangelicals: when going north of the border many of them still preferred to worship in the Presbyterian – and Established – Church of Scotland, and a CMS circular of the time continued to refer to the church in the USA as 'a separate and independent branch of the Church of Christ'.[4]

It was at this London meeting that the Australian and Canadian bishops began discussing not only their own self-government but proposals for a union of Protestant episcopal churches. This had the support of SPG, but in the event what happened was the 1867 meeting of Anglican bishops – the first Lambeth Conference – at the invitation of Archbishop Longley, prompted by the disquiet of Canadian bishops at the apparently heretical writings of John Colenso, Bishop of Natal from 1853.

There were by then 144 bishops around the world, all of them white men of European stock, but only 76 made it to Lambeth. Some stayed away, fearing that it would become a general synod of all the churches in full communion with the Church of England, despite Longley's assurance that 'No declaration of faith shall be made, and no decision come to which shall affect generally the interests of the Church, but that we shall meet together for brotherly counsel and encouragement.' The Dean of Westminster refused to host the closing service because of 'uncertainty as to the effect of its measures'. Even the Archbishop of York stayed at home, doubtful of the value of such a gathering. Nevertheless a second conference took place in 1878, and receiving an invitation came to be almost the definition of being part of the Communion. The most significant move to define Anglicanism itself was made at the third conference in 1888 which approved the 'Lambeth Quadrilateral', adapted from a proposal of the American House of

Bishops, as the basic criterion upon which reunion with another church might be undertaken:

> The Holy Scriptures of the Old and New Testaments, as 'containing all things necessary to salvation,' and as being the rule and ultimate standard of faith; The Apostles' Creed, as the Baptismal Symbol, and the Nicene Creed, as the sufficient statement of the Christian faith; The two Sacraments ordained by Christ Himself – Baptism and the Supper of the Lord – ministered with unfailing use of Christ's words of Institution, and of the elements ordained by Him; and The Historic Episcopate, locally adapted in the methods of its administration to the varying needs of the nations and peoples called of God into the Unity of His Church.[5]

It may be useful to say something here about the word 'Anglican'. Originally it just meant the Church in England, as in Magna Carta's *Ecclesia Anglicana*. This national identity was reinforced by the claims of the English Reformation for a (colonial) relationship between the nation and its church, and a (decolonial?) right for a national church to take charge of its own affairs – both are relevant to how other national churches see themselves within the Communion today. 'Anglican' then came to mean the church which had arrived from England, and it was only in the nineteenth century that it came to mean a distinctive 'branch' of Christianity and the family of churches who identify with it.[6]

A post-colonial Church?

We have already noted the new imperialism at the turn of the twentieth century which was both an expression of confidence in human progress, and a reaction against the growing tensions between imperial powers. In 1910 the leaders of the world's churches and missionary societies came together in Edinburgh for a conference on 'The Evangelization of the World in This Generation'. The UMCA shunned such a Protestant gathering, but SPG was more keen. This conference led to the creation of the International Missionary Council and, as its 1928 meeting in Jerusalem said, an increasing awareness of 'the new and true conception of the Christian missionary under-taking as a shared enterprise. Then all churches will be regarded as sending churches; and all churches will be regarded as receiving churches.'[7]

However, only 17 of the 1,200 delegates at Edinburgh were non-European. Among these was Samuel Azariah, a clergyman from south India who was to become the first Indian to be consecrated an Anglican bishop, in the Diocese of Dornakal. He was heckled by some of the white missionaries to India present, but as he pleaded for 'the foreign missionary to show that he is in the midst of the people to be to them not a lord and master but a brother and a friend', his words marked out the beginning of a new, non-colonial era. 'Through all the ages to come the Indian Church will rise up in gratitude to attest the heroism and self denying labors of the missionary body. You have given your goods to feed the poor. You have given your bodies to be burned. We ask for love. Give us friends.'[8]

A 'native episcopate' was slow to appear around the Communion, despite the call of the 1908 Lambeth Conference that:

> Every effort should be made to train native churches and congregations in self-support and self-government; and in view of the great importance of the establishment of a native episcopate in all countries where the Church is planted, this Conference urges the necessity of providing an advanced theological and practical training for the ablest of the native clergy in the mission field.[9]

The next Indian diocesan bishop after Azariah was appointed only in 1945, in the Diocese of Travancore and Cochin. The first appointment of a bishop in a CMS part of Africa took place in 1952, in Nigeria, and the first in a UMCA area in 1965, in Dar-es-Salaam. Malawi had to wait until 1981.

But the world was changing. European confidence, shaken by two world wars, was challenged by the emerging nations of the south. In the famous words of Che Guevara, 'The final hour of colonialism has struck, and millions of inhabitants of Africa, Asia and Latin America rise to meet a new life and demand their unrestricted right to self-determination.'[10] As Britain came to terms with the 'winds of change' which heralded the end of empire, so too did the Church of England as Archbishop Fisher, somewhat mirroring Prime Minister Harold Macmillan, created new Provinces, partly to avoid the detailed problems which otherwise came to him as Metropolitan, but also to distance the Church from colonial structures at this time of emerging resistance to them, especially in Africa. Some imperial ambitions continued: as late as the 1940s the British-born bishop in Ghana sought to win over members of other churches by using the slogan 'Join your King's Church',[11] and when Ian Smith made his Unilateral Declaration of Independence (UDI) in Southern Rhodesia in 1965 he claimed it as 'a blow for the preservation of justice, civilization, and Christianity'.

Such changes led some to think that the missionary era was also now finished: 'The age of missions is at an end; the age of mission has begun.'[12] Back in 1932 one of the reasons why the Harvard philosopher William Hocking had wanted to reduce Christianity to the social gospel rather than evangelism was that missionary movements were in alliance with Western imperialism. Now similar things were being heard from the newly independent churches, particularly through the World Council of Churches (WCC). At the WCC's 1966 'Church and Society' conference in Geneva Eduardo Mondlane, leader of the FRELIMO liberation movement in Mozambique, with a Marxist understanding of neo-colonialism, urged the churches to stop playing their part in international dependency. Its 1973 World Mission Conference in Bangkok defined 'salvation' as encompassing socio-political as well as spiritual aspects in equal measure.

In 1974 the All Africa Council of Churches – in a somewhat symbolic gesture – called for a moratorium on the supply of money and personnel as the only way to become 'truly and authentically ourselves while remaining a respected and responsible part of the Universal Church'.[13] Its General Secretary, Burgess Carr, demanded the abolition of missionary societies because they were the 'perpetuators of structural violence at the deepest level of our humanity in the so-called Younger Churches ... Their period of service is drawing to a close; the Churches of this world can together increasingly take up the considered responsibility of working together in the fullness of Christian witness and service to the world.'[14]

For Anglicans, this kind of thinking finally hit home at the Congress held in Toronto in 1963. There had been two previous Anglican Congresses, London in 1908 and Minneapolis in 1954. Toronto became famous for the breakthrough concerning 'Mutual Responsibility and

Interdependence in the Body of Christ', what it called in its final statement 'the rebirth of the Anglican Communion':

> The time has fully come when this unity and interdependence must find a completely new level of expression and corporate obedience . . . To use the words 'older' or 'younger' or 'sending' or 'receiving' with respect to churches is unreal and untrue in the world and in our Communion.[15]

In response the Bishop of Tokyo said:

> Formerly, a giver and receiver faced each other, each preoccupied with the reactions of the other, each ashamed, both with anxious eyes fastened on the gift. Now we are released from this, for we stand hand in hand facing the one great missionary task . . . where, before, some of us felt that we had no gifts because we were confronting those we thought had everything, now we shall discover that all have gifts that are needed and in giving we shall receive.[16]

Structures for Communion

Today the Anglican Communion comprises an estimated 80 million Christians, the majority of whom live in the South: 'If there is such a thing as an Average Anglican, she is 22, lives in sub-Saharan Africa, and must walk several kilometres a day to fetch water for her three or four children.'[17] They are members of 44 different churches spread across the globe: 34 Provinces, 4 United Churches, and 6 others. The largest is the 'Church of Nigeria (Anglican Communion)' with 166 dioceses, and growing.

Over time the Communion has developed four Instruments of Communion that serve this worldwide family of Anglican/Episcopal churches, the first being the Archbishop of Canterbury himself as the 'Focus for Unity'. Next comes the Lambeth Conference, which has met 14 times since 1867, roughly every ten years except when the two world wars intervened. In 1998, before some Provinces began absenting themselves, 749 bishops attended, including for the first time 11 women. Third, the Anglican Consultative Council (ACC) meets every three years or so, and is a more synodical body with members – bishops, clergy and laity – appointed by each Province. It first met in 1971, and most recently in Jamaica in 2009. Finally there is the Primates Meeting, established in 1978 by Donald Coggan (101st Archbishop of Canterbury) as an opportunity for 'leisurely thought, prayer and deep consultation'. It comprises the senior archbishops and bishops of the Communion, and has played a significant role in recent disputes.

Most of the Communion's activity is carried out through informal meetings and networks, but some more centralized programmes have been set up by the ACC, and are now detailed on the Anglican Communion Office website.[18] One is called 'Continuing Indaba', a development of the 'listening process' which was created to facilitate greater sharing of experience following the 1998 Conference resolution on gay and lesbian people. Also arising from the Communion's current problems is a new project on 'The Bible in the Life of the Church'.[19] There is also TEAC (Theological Education in the Anglican Communion), which has usefully defined the Anglican Way by four 'signposts': Formed by Scripture, Shaped by Worship, Ordered for Communion, and Directed by God's Mission.[20]

For a long time the Communion rested on the 'bonds of affection' arising from its shared history and the four Instruments of Communion, which enabled the autonomous churches which had emerged to continue to belong together. The 1930 Lambeth Conference restated 'the principle of the autonomy of particular Churches based upon a common faith and order': they were, it said, 'bound together not by a central legislative and executive authority, but by mutual loyalty sustained through the common counsel of the bishops in conference'.[21]

However, the tensions which came to a head at the 1998 Lambeth Conference (see Chapter 3) led to calls for something more, and these tensions reached crisis point in 2003. A special Primates Meeting was called following events in North America: the election of a bishop in an openly gay partnership, and moves in one Canadian diocese to officially bless same-sex partnerships. The result was the 'Windsor Process',[22] culminating in a proposal for an Anglican Covenant. At the time of writing the proposed Covenant, in its final (2009) draft, has been sent to all the Provinces, and their responses will be considered at the next meeting of the Anglican Consultative Council (ACC 15) in 2012. It says that it seeks to 'respect the constitutional autonomy of all of the Churches of the Anglican Communion, while upholding our mutual responsibility and interdependence in the Body of Christ, and the responsibility of each to the Communion as a whole'.[23] Its most controversial part deals with the need for consultation and restraint by churches seeking to do what may be perceived by others as controversial or new. It has been suggested that those who ignore this may cease to be full members of the Communion – what Archbishop Rowan Williams has called the 'two track model'.[24]

Does the Anglican Communion need more formulae than the Lambeth Quadrilateral? Are the four Instruments of Communion now insufficient? Its own Theological and Doctrinal Commission first raised the question in its 1997 Virginia Report: 'There is a question as to whether effective communion, at all levels, does not require appropriate instruments, with due safeguards, not only for legislation, but also for oversight. Is not universal authority a necessary corollary of universal communion?'[25]

Rowan Williams speaks of the Covenant 'translating [our] underlying sacramental communion into a more effective institutional reality'. Most Anglican leaders in the South clearly believe that this is needed, and urgently, to save the Communion from splitting or becoming just a federation of churches. Some of them would like to see the role of the Primates Meeting strengthened 'to exercise an enhanced responsibility in offering guidance on doctrinal, moral and pastoral matters'.[26] When the leaders from 20 Anglican Provinces met in Singapore in April 2010 for the fourth 'Anglican South to South Encounter' they stated: 'we believe that all those who adopt the Covenant must be in compliance with Lambeth I.10 and in particular its insistence that homosexual practice is incompatible with Scripture'.[27]

Other responses are more cautious, believing that the Covenant threatens what it means to be an Anglican. They fear that it would turn the Communion into a 'confessional' church, and member churches would be handing over decision making to an external body. Bruce Kaye shares Rowan Williams's commitment to a gospel catholicity, but seeks something more conciliar – global models of connection and facilitating networks – rather than the demand for institutional affiliation which the Covenant could become.[28] If the Trinity is about '*perichoresis*', that is, mutual interchange, he says, then 'any ecclesiology must begin with God who creates community'.[29] The first response of the Church in Wales was to call for the Covenant to be less legalistic and more relational.[30] In November 2010 the Church of England General Synod agreed to refer it to the dioceses, despite a media campaign led by the lobbying group Inclusive Church. At this group's 2009 Conference a retired bishop, Peter Selby, had denounced it as an attempt to centralize and homogenize the Church.[31] An Old Testament scholar doubts whether what Scripture means by Covenant should in any case be used in this way.[32]

3

The Anglican Communion today

It's depressing that the Anglican Communion has become synonymous with talk of disagreement and the threat of schism. Those of us who are privileged to spend time around the world with our fellow Anglicans will want to begin by telling a much more positive story, and I recount some of these stories in Chapter 5. These people don't wake up every morning wondering which side they should take in the homosexuality debate. They have enough to do just getting on with the job of being a Christian in their particular situation and taking up what they believe is their part in God's mission. Even when bishops meet and synods gather, their main business is about staying faithful and meeting the challenges in the place where God has called them to be the Church.

It is by and large only on the international stage that the problems become public. This was true from the beginning: the first meeting of bishops at a Lambeth Conference happened because of the upset caused by the writings of Bishop Colenso in South Africa, which questioned eternal damnation and the infallibility of Scripture. What's also interesting about the Colenso episode is that, like more recent disputes, there was much more going on underneath the surface. It raised questions of biblical authority and church discipline at a time when missionary work overseas was meant to provide an escape from such post-Enlightenment pressures at home. It forced the issue, very much raised by the Tractarians since Keble, about who should make decisions about the life and doctrine of the Church. And it began to raise questions about colonialism, for government, especially in the confusion as to whether authority now lay in London or Cape Town, and for the Church. How should such matters be resolved?

In summoning the 1867 Conference Archbishop Longley was quite clear that 'it would not be competent to make declarations or lay down definitions on points of doctrine',[1] and in the event the reports on the Colenso affair were simply received and referred to any future Conference for action.

The growth of dissent

The presenting issues in our current turmoils began with the ordination of women, and went on to encompass wider areas of human sexuality. Up to this point the Communion had found ways of coping with such potentially divisive situations.[2] On divorce, the Lambeth Conference of 1920 reiterated the indissolubility of marriage, but since then has restricted itself to promoting marriage and family life, perhaps because divorce itself is now seen very differently in different parts of the Communion. Polygamy could well have separated parts of Africa from the rest of the Communion, but the 1988 Conference accepted the compromise that a polygamist might be baptized and not have to put away any of his wives if his community was content with the situation and he did not marry again. On the issue of contraception, successive Lambeth Conferences have shown a remarkable ability to meet changing perceptions: in 1920 it was rejected outright, even within marriage, but by 1958 it had become a recommended part of 'responsible parenthood'.

In 1978, the bishops coming to the Lambeth Conference had to deal with the fact that in 1974 the Diocese of Philadelphia had ordained 11 women to the priesthood, and two years later the General Convention had authorized the ordination of women throughout the Episcopal Church. But the result was not schism but accommodation. This was all the more remarkable because such ordinations were an issue which for Catholics touched on the very essence of the Church, the validity of its ministry and thereby its sacraments, and one where for some evangelicals Scripture explicitly barred women from such ministry. The previous Conference in 1968 had sought patience and restraint on this contentious issue where there was no common mind. However, the 1978 consensus was to allow diverse practice – albeit with talk of alternative episcopal arrangements for those opposed – or at least to agree to disagree. Since then, 28 of the 38 Provinces have resolved to ordain women priests, although some of these, and particularly the Church of England, have struggled with how to open the episcopate to women without totally alienating those who are opposed. One route continued to discriminate against women, the other created in effect two churches. Failure to find such a principled way forward led the Church in Wales in 2008 to decide not to proceed.

The Episcopal Church in the USA, however, was already on the way to having women bishops by the time the 1988 Lambeth Conference met, and once again the stability of the Communion was under threat. This led to the Virginia Report,[3] which attempted to put the ecclesiological issues of both ministry itself and the Communion's interdependence into a more theological, trinitarian, framework. Some felt that this necessitated a rather over-structural understanding of the Trinity, with the loss of the more relational and innovatory aspects which the Communion might also need to reflect.

However, another and more intractable issue was coming to the fore, and again from North America: the blessing of same-sex partnerships, and the ordination of people living openly in them. In the period before the 1998 Lambeth Conference the battle lines were beginning to be drawn. The more conservative leaders of the Communion had got together in Kuala Lumpur, Dallas and Kampala. At the Dallas meeting, Stephen Noll, the American who was to become Vice-Chancellor of Uganda Christian University, acknowledged that homosexuality was not a significant issue for Anglicans from the South, but warned that unless they helped their Northern colleagues now it would soon spread to them. 'Come over and help us,' he urged, echoing the missionary call in both the Acts of the Apostles and the founding of SPG.

At Lambeth itself, the sub-section on Human Sexuality laboured long and hard to produce a unanimous report. The result was a quintessentially Anglican document, asserting what we held in common, acknowledging that in many places we held different views, and committing the Communion to continue working and travelling together.

It was a different story on the floor of the Conference plenary. Our report was accepted, but the following resolution was hardened up, including the addition of the now notorious rejection of homosexual practice as 'incompatible with Scripture'. It did, however, retain the statement that homosexual persons are 'loved by God and that all baptized, believing and faithful persons, regardless of sexual orientation, are full members of the Body of Christ', and an amendment was added calling for their experience to be listened to.

Many in the Episcopal Church were shocked but undaunted. In 2003 they elected Gene Robinson, a divorced man living in an open and committed same-sex partnership, as Bishop of New Hampshire, and a majority of other dioceses, meeting at General Convention, gave their consent. Subsequent events have showed that however vocal the opposition, some of whom want to leave the Episcopal Church altogether, the majority of American Episcopalians are not opposed to such developments and many give them enthusiastic welcome. In 2009 the Diocese of Massachusetts Synod called for same-sex marriages, now part of Massachusetts State law, to be solemnized in church: no one spoke against it, and a month later the Bishop allowed it.

The response of the wider Communion to what was going on in the USA, and to some extent in Canada as well, was the publication of the Windsor Report in 2004.[4] Spurred on by angry meetings of the Primates, its main recommendation was for a Covenant that would in some way define the parameters of Anglicanism and determine what should happen to those who were considered to have departed from it. By the time of the 2008 Lambeth Conference this was in its third public draft, and most attention was being paid to the final section where the disciplinary mechanisms were set out. There was talk at Lambeth of a two-track Communion, according to what a Province decided to do, in particular, about the homosexual issue. But before that the Covenant itself will need to be put before every Province, and the signs are that many have grave doubts as to whether this is an appropriate way to define Anglicanism or determine membership of the Communion.

Many of the conservatives have found this process of correcting – they might say 'purifying' – the Communion far too slow. In the summer of 2008, just before the Lambeth Conference, they organized the Global Anglican Future Conference (GAFCON) in Jerusalem. Their Declaration, and the follow-up movement, the Fellowship of Confessing Anglicans (FCA), is about reforming the Anglican Communion 'around the biblical gospel'. Its Primates Council now includes Nigeria, West Africa, Rwanda, Tanzania, Kenya, Uganda and the Southern Cone.

A month later, the Lambeth Conference met in Canterbury, but without the African Provinces who had decided to boycott it. At least three Church of England bishops also stayed away. No official list of participants was ever issued, perhaps to protect those bishops whose attendance might have offended either their government or their archbishop, but it's thought that 230 bishops, mainly from Africa, declined the invitation. Their reasons were clearly set forward in the statement 'The Road to Lambeth' from the Council of Anglican Provinces in Africa (CAPA): 'We will definitely not attend any Lambeth Conference to which the violators of the Lambeth Resolution [I.10] are also invited as participants or observers.'

This was a very different Lambeth Conference from 1998: there were no plenary resolutions, but rather an *indaba* process (described in the final Reflections document as 'an African ideal of purposeful discussion on the common concerns of our shared life') of Bible study and meeting. While open hearings did consider the contentious issues, it was left to the Archbishop of Canterbury to chart the way forward. In so doing he reinforced the need for three moratoria. The first two required restraint on the blessing of same-sex partnerships and on the ministry, perhaps especially episcopal ministry, of people in such partnerships. The third moratorium concerned crossing Provincial boundaries, causing anguish from some African and Southern Cone bishops convinced that the faithful remnant in the United States needed their pastoral care.

The response of the Episcopal Church was initially to agree to some constraint, while pointing out that bishops from other Provinces were continuing to transgress their jurisdiction. But their 2009 General Convention indicated a determination to continue moving forward, and in 2010 they accepted the election of Canon Mary Glasspool, living in a twenty-year partnership with another woman, as a suffragan bishop in the Diocese of Los Angeles.

This led more American dioceses to consider leaving the Episcopal Church altogether. The breakaway movement had begun in early 2000 when Chuck Murphy and John Rodgers were consecrated missionary bishops for what became the Anglican Mission in the Americas, taking its authority from the Province of Rwanda. In April 2007 the Primate of Nigeria appointed his own bishop for North America, and later that year the Uganda church consecrated a US bishop to oversee many of the US parishes that it supports.

There were various movements to bring dissident groups together, such as the Anglican Communion Network and Common Cause, and some linking up with the Province of the Southern Cone. Finally, in June 2009 one of the breakaway bishops, Robert Duncan of Pittsburgh, led the creation of what claims to be a new Province of the Anglican Communion, independent of TEC: the Anglican Church of North America. Duncan became an archbishop, and now sits with the GAFCON/FCA Primates.

America's civil war

Christianity is not by nature a formulaic religion. For example, there has always been a tension between those who emphasize the sinfulness of humanity, the Cross of Christ and the need for personal salvation, and those who stress human goodness, the Incarnation of Jesus and the need for service and justice. Such things are not absolutes or alternatives, but the priority they have been accorded has often reflected the age or culture in which the Church was to be found. Apart from the time of its own Civil War in the seventeenth century, Anglicanism has been particularly adept at holding such differences together, from the politically motivated *via media* of the English Reformation to the development of a more nuanced 'comprehensiveness' in recent Anglican theology. It is this which is being challenged by current events.

Rowan Williams has characterized our present difficulties as the conflict between a 'frozen traditionalism' and a 'bland and essentially secular inclusivity'.[5] This is nowhere more evident than in what can be called the Episcopal Church's 'civil war', and one which has real echoes of the issues behind that nation's Civil War in the nineteenth century. This is not to suggest that there are only two sides to this debate, or only two parties in the Episcopal Church, any more than that there is one dividing line between the North (or, the West) and the Global South. But there is here, especially when seen through the lens of post-modern thinking, a clear two-way movement: one claiming to return to pre-modernism, and one seeking to embrace quite new ways of thinking, and both in their way challenging traditional Anglicanism.

First, the conservatives. They would prefer to be called 'traditionalists', but that already begs the initial question: is this a conservationist movement, wedded to preserving both inherited moral norms (whether or not that is what mission is about) and traditional Anglicanism (whether or not that is the way forward in post-colonial cultures), or does it have more in common than it would like to admit with other contemporary developments which it eschews?

Karen Armstrong's work on fundamentalism suggests that such conservative religious movements are more the children of modernity than a return to something that existed before.[6] Pre-modernity, she argues, knew the difference between myth (that which gives meaning) and more empirical facts, but when modern Western society lost the sense of *mythos* and enshrined *logos* as its foundation, mythical narratives and the rituals and meanings attached to them ceded authority to that which is rational, pragmatic and scientific. Articles of faith and sacred texts became objectified.

In the case of Anglican conservatives, this may be especially seen in their claims for biblical authority. Anglicans have never believed in biblical inerrancy, but only that 'Holy Scripture containeth all things necessary to salvation'[7] and is 'the rule and ultimate standard of faith'.[8] So if phrases like 'incompatible with Scripture' in Resolution I.10 of Lambeth 1998 suggest the reading of Scripture 'without interpretation' – that is, without the benefit of tradition and reason – this raises serious questions about its Anglican credentials. Other critics would argue that Anglicanism has never been this kind of 'confessing tradition' anyway – it is rooted in common prayer rather than common beliefs.

Nevertheless it is the claim of bodies like GAFCON and the conservative lobby group 'Anglican Mainstream' which helped create it, that they are returning the Communion to Bible-based orthodoxy. 'We now have people in the US but not only there who believe things about God, about salvation, about marriage and about human sexuality that seem to be another religion,' said Bishop Michael Nazir-Ali as he resigned from the Diocese of Rochester.[9] Peter Jensen, Archbishop of Sydney, and a leading light of FCA, denies that it's homophobic: 'What we see in the goings-on in New Hampshire and elsewhere is, if you like, a symbolic enactment of a different set of ideas. . . . It is not so much the thing itself, as what it represents in our church which has so alarmed us.'[10]

Coming from the other direction are the liberals (who again would prefer a different name, such as inclusivists or progressives). Here I need to add some personal explanation, because much of this book was written during a guest scholarship at the Episcopal Divinity School which is proudly at the cutting edge of this movement within the Episcopal Church. I am on the liberal side with regard to ethical issues such as economic justice and human sexuality, but more traditional when it comes to doctrine and spirituality, so it was a challenging experience, in this wonderfully hospitable institution, to be part of a community where the commitment to 'Justice, Compassion and Reconciliation' appears more prominent than inherited statements of faith, and where, at the installation of the new Dean, her celebration of being the first woman in an openly lesbian partnership to head a seminary was greeted by whoops of delight.

Underlying much of this more inclusivist theology is what postmodernists call a 'deconstructionist' reading of literature. This allows those who have not played much part in the story up to now – the poor, the marginalized and the colonized – to find their own voice and indeed to find themselves addressed and included in the biblical promises of liberation.[11] It's sometimes called reading Scripture 'from below'. However, this also makes the study of Scripture a much more subjective exercise because the new significance given to the reader or hearer can make his or her experience as authoritative as the text itself, especially if that reader or hearer feels alienated from what has been the mainstream.

This is particularly seen in the deep influence of feminist theology in this part of the Episcopal Church, where the disinclination to use words like kingdom, Judge and even Lord, is about more than wanting to embrace the feminine side of God. For some, much definition of sin, and therefore many constructs of atonement, arise from a masculine – indeed, colonial – understanding of human and divine power which needs to be corrected.

Emotions run high on both sides. Traditionalists claim that the others have deserted orthodox Christianity and replaced it with a theology which 'reflects the soft syncretism of modernity watched over by a benign and indulgent God who allows all kinds of moral compromise for the sake of inclusivity'.[12] One parody of Episcopalian liturgy is that it now reflects not so much the rehearsal of salvation history and the people's response in worship and penitence, but more a self-affirmation: 'God, I just want you to know that being a Christian helps me feel really good about myself.' Ephraim Radner, a conservative scholar who has stayed in the Episcopal Church, rather turns the tables on the liberals when he says that they have bought into 'our commodified culture of individualistic atomization'[13] and removed the challenge which the Church ought to be making to this, and to the consumer capitalism which results from it.

The other side point to the way that God is putting right centuries of injustice, and how a promise made by a previous Presiding Bishop that 'There shall be no outcasts'[14] is finally coming true. They point to how Jesus welcomed everyone, and especially those who were poor or deemed to be impure: he opposed those who, like today's conservatives, used religion to exclude such people. They say that churches which welcome gay and lesbian people are growing and attracting young families in which the parents want their children to grow up in a society where no one is put down or thrown out.

The ultra-liberal Bishop John Shelby Spong has now lost all patience with the other side:

> I will no longer listen to televised debates conducted by 'fair-minded' channels that seek to give 'both sides' of this issue 'equal time.' I am aware that these stations no longer give equal time to the advocates of treating women as if they are the property of men or to the advocates of reinstating either segregation or slavery, despite the fact that when these evil institutions were coming to an end the Bible was still being quoted frequently on each of these subjects. . . . I will no longer be

respectful of the leadership of the Archbishop of Canterbury, who seems to believe that rude behaviour, intolerance and even killing prejudice is somehow acceptable, so long as it comes from third-world religious leaders, who more than anything else reveal in themselves the price that colonial oppression has required of the minds and hearts of so many of our world's population. I see no way that ignorance and truth can be placed side by side, nor do I believe that evil is somehow less evil if the Bible is quoted to justify it.[15]

Human sexuality

Our concern here is not homosexuality itself, with which I tried to deal in a book after the 1998 Lambeth Conference,[16] but rather how and why homosexuality has become, for those on both sides of the debate, such a central issue for Anglicans, and almost the touchstone on which Christian faithfulness is to be assessed. I made the wry suggestion in the *Journal of Anglican Studies* that Resolution I.10 'has extended the Lambeth Quadrilateral to a Pentagon, in both the geometric and military senses!'[17] It would appear that for people on every side of the debate, the pressures of their home culture have played an important part.

Maybe for the conservatives it was the only issue available. In their determination to reaffirm what they believe to be Christian orthodoxy, there are other issues on which Scripture (or at least, St Paul) is very clear, such as divorce and remarriage, or the role of women in both society and church, but these would have involved tackling US culture head-on, and indeed would have alienated many of their own members. It's instructive that in the 2009 canons of the newly formed Anglican Church of North America, there is direct provision for marriage after divorce, and the ordination of women is treated as a secondary matter despite its significance for the validity of ministry.

How far the conservatives had to convince their potential allies in the South about the centrality of the homosexual issue is another interesting question.[18] If homosexuality as a clearly identified status, and even as a word, only emerged in Europe in the late nineteenth century, it does not seem to have featured in public discourse in most of the South until the coming of the colonizers and their laws against it.[19] This may not be surprising when welfare and even survival depended on marriage and family networks.

In the post-colonial world homosexuality has become something of a weapon with which to beat Western decadence. The condemnation of homosexuals has served to assert, especially where Islam is strong, that Christianity is not a foreign import but part of the local culture. Church leaders in Uganda and Nigeria have shown little willingness to criticize government legislation against gay people. In Zimbabwe the bishops ousted for their corruption and support of government injustices have tried to claim that their opponents were pro-gay.

Miranda Hassett talks of how an exchange was taking place.[20] The conservative minorities in the USA needed not just the numbers which Anglicans in the South could provide, but also their moral authority and spiritual capital. Their youthful zeal could be compared with declining churches in the West, even if that meant some romanticizing of their poverty and suffering. What role has money played in this exchange? This is a sensitive issue, but two things are probably true: funding did not determine the moral stance that church leaders in the South have taken, but nevertheless a great deal of support has flowed their way in return.[21] Jim Naughton from the Episcopal Diocese of Washington,[22] and Kapya Kaoma,[23] an Anglican priest from Zambia, have traced the influence and funding which has come from right-wing and homophobic organizations in the United States to church leaders in Nigeria, Uganda and Kenya.

Equally one must ask, why has homosexuality become such an issue for US liberals? Part of the answer goes back to the founding philosophy of American independence: rationalism, anti-colonialism, and the inalienable right of the individual to choose his or her own way of life and belief. It took some time – and much bloodshed in the Civil War – for such freedoms to be extended beyond the white (male) settlers, but the Civil Rights movement of the last century shaped much that has followed. First it was racial equality – not that the followers of Martin Luther King saw much in common between their cause and gay liberation – and then women's rights. The Episcopal Church moved via the ordination of women to the cause of gay and lesbian people: according to Gayle Harris, a black woman bishop in the Diocese of Massachusetts, 'As a person who knows what it means to be oppressed, I refuse to allow my brothers and sisters in the faith to be discriminated against.'[24] She sees the full inclusion of gay people as a matter of justice, correcting the judgemental exclusiveness of the Church, and as a further step in putting into practice the promise of Jesus to let the oppressed go free.

But the fact that this issue has come to such prominence also reflects the closeness of the Episcopal Church to political liberalism, especially now the Democratic Party, and the lifestyle which most Episcopalians enjoy. It's a very US culture of extroversion, romanticism and emotionalism which at its best makes people wonderfully open and hospitable, and at worst leads to neurosis. It treasures personal choice and individuality. It may be noteworthy that the inhabitants of New England inherited from the Pilgrim Fathers not so much their moral Puritanism as their commitment to dissent and independence, which may be why the first openly gay bishop is to be found in New Hampshire.

Arising from this same history there is the different 'political' outlook of Americans, which is reflected in the polity of the Episcopal Church. Their 1979 Baptismal Covenant, while reflecting a return to more biblical models of church, has also reinforced a cultural emphasis on individual freedom and self-expression. And that suspicion which independently minded settlers had about bishops and colonial control is still evident today when Anglican Communion bodies try to tell them what to do, or assume that their presiding bishop has the power which many other Primates can exercise.

So Americans have their own post-colonial identity, however much other parts of the world may accuse them of acting colonially today. Bringing this all together, we may note a couple of interesting 'post-colonial' paradoxes. First, it is the conservatives from the southern states, historically not very aware of the wider world and the more racially segregated, who have been willing to see the global picture and even put themselves under black leadership. It is the liberals who played such a large part in the development of a global Church who have been willing to scandalize the rest of the Communion, often giving the impression that sooner or later the rest of the world will see that they are right.

Second, America and Africa are very conscious of their slave trade inheritance. An increasing number of North Americans see gay liberation as a further act of emancipation: a programme from Vermont directly links that diocese's previous complicity with slavery, and the use of Scripture to defend it, with the lobby at General Convention to bless same-sex partnerships.[25] However, when West Africans remember what the transatlantic slave trade did to their forebears they are more likely to see the imposition of gay liberation as a continuing attempt by those with (imperial) power to control their lives. Bishop Bernard Ntahoturi of Burundi responded to the comments of Gayle Harris cited above with: 'You cannot compare slavery with homosexuality. Slavery is a sin. Homosexuality is not about rights, it's about how God created you.'[26]

Finally, one might ask what has happened to another moral issue: economic justice, which should surely be at the top of the Christian agenda, but which has received little priority from Western Anglicans, whether conservative or liberal. Scripture takes this far more seriously than sexuality, and until fairly recently the tradition of the Church took an equally hard line on such matters as usury. The liberals, despite General Convention's commitment to the Millennium Development Goals and the emergence of Anglicans for Global Reconciliation, have done little to distance themselves from US capitalism and its economic colonialism. The conservatives, having derailed the 1998 Lambeth Conference from its planned focus on international debt, have equally said very little on the matter apart from some half-hearted support for their Five Talents micro-finance initiative.

So have the church leaders in the South allowed themselves to be sidetracked on to Western ethical agendas rather than struggling for the kind of economic changes which might meet the crying needs of their own people? Certainly Bishop Trevor Mwamba of Botswana believes that the integrity of people outside the northern hemisphere has been degraded by concentration on the gay and lesbian debate at the expense of more immediate and pressing issues such as poverty, disease, bad governance and the environment. 'Africa does not want the sexuality debate imposed upon it as a priority agenda. Our priority is about basic survival.'[27]

Where now?

We have looked at the problems and divisions which beset the Anglican Communion. The picture is complex and fluid, but underlying it we might see the following. The post-imperial inheritance from the Church of England is cherished by many, but is also suspect in both North America and in the Global South. In a Communion such as ours the effects of post-colonialism are unavoidable, but in the new alliances and patterns of support which are emerging there is the danger of creating new colonial dependencies. There are questions about how the liberals are embracing post-modernism and whether the conservatives are actually as traditionalist as they claim. After we have stood back and considered, in Chapter 4, what the terms 'mission' and 'Anglican' actually mean, we shall look in Chapter 5 at how all this impacts, more practically, on mission around the Anglican Communion. Then, in Chapter 6, we return to what the more theoretical tools of post-modernism, post-imperialism and post-colonialism may be able to show us, before looking, in a final chapter, to possible futures.

4

The mission of God and the Anglican tradition

The Missio Dei

The *Missio Dei* or 'Mission of God' is God's self-revelation as the One who loves the world and is actively involved in and with the world. It embraces both Church and world, and the Church is privileged to be called to participate in God's mission. Or in the words of the last century's great missiologist, David Bosch: 'To participate in mission is to participate in the movement of God's love toward people, since God is a fountain of sending love.'[1]

Twentieth-century theology, reacting against the more rationalistic theology which resulted from the Enlightenment, put the emphasis back on the initiative of God, rather than seeing mission as primarily a human activity. This found particular expression in the work of Karl Barth, to whom the concept of *Missio Dei*, if not the exact words, is often attributed.

So the Willingen Statement from the 1952 meeting of the International Missionary Council said that mission must be first and foremost God's mission. It went on to say that we can only understand this Mission of God in terms of the triune character of God. It is in the very nature of God to give and receive, to send and return, fundamentally to love the other, and where this overflows in the world, in creation, in Christ, and ultimately in the consummation of all things in Christ, we see the Mission of God, the work of God, and the self-revelation of God himself (herself/themselves).

And we are called to join in, as we discover what God is doing and seek to reflect who God is. This raises the question of where the

Church fits into the *Missio Dei*. The Willingen Statement was clear that 'the Missionary Calling of the Church is derived from the mission of God': the Church has a missionary calling rather than a mission, and that calling is to engage in God's mission. Our mission therefore has no life of its own; only in the hands of the sending God can it truly be called mission, because the missionary initiative comes from God alone. The Church is both part of what God is doing, as a particular expression or embodiment of the work of God flowing from the very nature of God, and has a particular vocation to engage with God in this work, in and for the world. In the words of Jürgen Moltmann, 'It is not the church that has a mission of salvation to fulfil in the world; it is the mission of the Son and the Spirit through the Father that includes the church.'[2]

In USPG's own theological statement we have focused on the concept of 'Communion' (*koinonia*) as a way of speaking about such things. We say:

> Communion is at the heart of God, the very life of the Trinity.
> God yearns to draw each one of us into this communion with him.
> It is in communion with God that we know and are known, we love and are loved.
> Communion is God's gift to the Church.
> We respond in worship, most of all when this communion is made real in the Eucharist.
> The Church is called to be the sign, foretaste and anticipation of God's mission.
> We are called to support each other as we engage in this mission wherever God has called us to be his Church.
> Communion is God's will and desire for all humanity and the whole of creation.
> Mission is therefore 'holistic', responding to all of God's liberating activity so that people may 'grow spiritually, thrive physically, and have a voice in an unjust world'.[3]

Focusing in this way on the *Missio Dei* means that we must exercise greater care when we use the word 'mission', and especially when we talk about the 'mission of the Church'. When I was invited to the Missions Conference of the Episcopal Church in the USA in 2008 they asked me to make a contribution on 'The Overseas Mission of the Episcopal Church'. My short response was that it shouldn't have one! Partly because, as we've just said, it is God who has a mission, not the Church, but also because a proper understanding of the *Missio Dei* means that mission can no longer be seen as the activity of one church acting overseas or in another culture. The frontier of mission is no longer primarily a geographical one. Indeed, what we have been saying about the *Missio Dei* raises fundamental questions about the kind of imperialism that shaped mission in the colonial age, where mission was about moving from the world that immediately surrounded the Church to beyond the frontiers of the empire(s) of Christendom. It also questions new and more contemporary imperialisms – geopolitical, economic and intellectual – which can appear to be shaping mission in our own day.

This shift away from such Christendom-rooted thinking was described by the 1963 conference of the Commission on World Mission and Evangelism, meeting in Mexico, in this way: the missionary frontier now runs around the world, it is the line which separates belief from unbelief, the unseen frontier which cuts across other frontiers and presents the universal Church with its primary missionary challenge. So the *Missio Dei* both challenges each one of us with the need to do mission in our own situation, and also causes us to rethink how we relate what we're doing with how the rest of the world Church is responding.

In *Transforming Mission*, David Bosch summarized how people had seen mission in the past:

> During preceding centuries mission was understood in a variety of ways. Sometimes it was interpreted primarily in soteriological terms: as saving individuals from eternal damnation. Or it was understood in cultural terms: as introducing people from the East and the South to the blessings and privileges of the Christian West. Often it was perceived in ecclesiastical categories: as the expansion of the church (or of a specific denomination).

He went on to describe the new emphases within *Missio Dei*:

> Mission was understood as being derived from the very nature of God. It was thus put in the context of the doctrine of the Trinity, not of ecclesiology or soteriology. The classical doctrine on the *Missio*

41

Dei as God the Father sending the Son, and God the Father and the Son sending the Spirit was expanded to include yet another 'movement': The Father, Son and the Holy Spirit sending the church into the world. As far as missionary thinking was concerned, this linking with the doctrine of the Trinity constituted an important innovation . . . Our mission has no life of its own: only in the hands of the sending God can it truly be called mission. Not least since the missionary initiative comes from God alone . . . Mission is thereby seen as a movement from God to the world; the church is viewed as an instrument for that mission. There is church because there is mission, not vice versa.[4]

John V. Taylor warned against this 'gloriously inclusive term' becoming too wide: 'There is an inherent, if not deliberate vagueness in the term "Mission of God" which lays it open to abuse. It can be made to include anything under the sun that anyone considers a Good Thing.'[5] This may be true, but it's also this very inclusiveness which can guard against the two ways in which some parts of the Church have chosen to misinterpret the *Missio Dei*.

The first, and partly in reaction to its Barthian origins, has been to put all the emphasis on the worldly context of the *Missio Dei* and to see God's engagement in the world as primarily humanistic. This rather modalist God, stripped of any real Trinitarian character or relationship, creates the world, identifies with it in Jesus, and remains active in it through the Spirit who blows wherever he (or she) wills. The Law is not so much transformed by grace as replaced by a new kind of good works. Programmes like the World Council of Churches' 'The World Sets the Agenda' – which I have to say profoundly influenced my own training and early ministry – are often accused of having reinforced this trend. It is found in the critique which liberation theology makes of even the global and holistic agenda of someone like David Bosch. It is seen today in many Christian charities, and in development agencies who have much to say about 'life before death' but without any larger context of life beyond it. It assesses the Church not as part of the activity of God but in terms of whether it can deliver certain goods.

In the opposing corner is the second direction in which *Missio Dei* may be said to have been misinterpreted, where the emphasis on God's initiative and agency is taken to mean that only those who are in conscious relationship with Christ or his Church can be caught up in it. For some, this leads to the more evangelical/charismatic belief that God only works, or at least works most effectively, through those who have in some way been 'born again' or who are filled with the Spirit. For others, the role of the Church is so understood within the *Missio Dei* as to see little or none of God's activity beyond its confines. This may be particularly evident where a more Catholic or Orthodox ecclesiology overplays the Church as the ark of salvation.

The Five Marks of Mission

One way of putting some of this into practical form, and of avoiding what I have suggested could be distorting directions, has been the Five Marks of Mission.[6] Although these originated within the Anglican Communion, they have been adopted far more widely, perhaps more in Protestant than Catholic circles, and for many people they provide a template for how the Church is engaging with the *Missio Dei*.

The first thing to say about the Five Marks of Mission is that they begin with the statement: 'the mission of the Church is the mission of Christ'.[7] If we see the *Missio Dei* as the overflowing of God into the world, nowhere is that more evident and more effectual than in the life, death and resurrection of Jesus.

The Five Marks can be seen as holding together the various aspects of mission:

1 To proclaim the Good News of the Kingdom.
2 To teach, baptize and nurture new believers.
3 To respond to human need by loving service.
4 To seek to transform unjust structures of society.

And, added a little later:

5 To strive to safeguard the integrity of creation and sustain and renew the life of the earth.

Many churches find these Five Marks a useful check list for their engagement in mission. But they are not without their dangers. The Anglican Communion's own Commission in Mission (Missio), meeting in Ely in 1996, raised some of these dangers.[8] First, as we've already noted, the Five Marks must not obscure the fact that it's God's mission not ours. Then, do they sufficiently take into account the different contexts in which churches find themselves? Next, do they take seriously enough the life of the churches themselves? For we are called to be not just doers of mission but a people of mission: that is, says the report, 'we are learning to allow every dimension of church life to be shaped and directed by our identity as a sign, foretaste and instrument of God's reign in Christ'.

Within this comes that central activity in the life of the Church – our worship. To quote the Missio report again,

> worship is not just something we do alongside our witness to the good news: worship is itself a witness to the world. It is a sign that all of life is holy, that hope and meaning can be found in offering ourselves to God (cf. Romans 12:1). And each time we celebrate the Eucharist, we proclaim Christ's death until he comes (1 Cor. 11:26). Our liturgical life is a vital dimension of our mission calling; and although it is not included in the Five Marks, it undergirds the forms of public witness listed there.

That takes us back to David Bosch, and how in his 'Transforming Mission' he added 'poiesis' – the need for beauty and for worship – to the standard duo of theory and praxis.[9]

So, returning to the Five Marks of Mission, some have wanted to add more marks acknowledging the life, and the worship, of the Church. Others, like Titus Presler in his Ten Marks of Mission, want to stress qualities rather than programmes.[10] Interestingly, the Anglican Consultative Council, meeting in Jamaica in 2009, sought a different sixth mark, on reconciliation. It endorsed a request from the Anglican Church of Canada, and from the Mutual Responsibility and Mission Consultation in Costa Rica, to add one relating to peace, conflict transformation and reconciliation. We will have to wait and see how this develops.

But there is something still more fundamental to say about the Five Marks, which takes us back to the nature of the *Missio Dei*: how do we interpret the first mark, and is it just one among five or do the rest follow from it and depend upon it? That 1996 report from the Anglican Communion commission[11] said that the first mark of mission, which was

> identified at [the sixth meeting of the Anglican Consultative Council] with personal evangelism, is really a summary of what all mission is about, because it is based on Jesus' own summary of his mission (Matthew 4:17, Mark 1:14–15, Luke 4:18, Luke 7:22; cf. John 3:14–17). Instead of being just one (albeit the first) of five distinct activities, this should be the key statement about everything we do in mission.

There is some truth in that if it means that all the marks are to be seen as part of proclaiming the good news of the kingdom, but not if the first mark is to be reduced to just personal evangelism.

So we are back at the questions: what is God doing in the world and where does it connect with the response of the individual and the life of the Church? The answer to these questions will determine how we engage in mission – including, crucially, how we relate to people of other faiths – and therefore what kind of mission activities we set up.

Let me illustrate this. The thinking that has gone on in USPG over recent years has led us to three central emphases. The first is holistic mission. So all the issues raised above about the interpretation and interrelationship of the Five Marks of Mission, and what may need adding to them, come into play. What I would want to affirm here is our belief that the witness of Scripture to the activity of God – in creation, through the saving acts of Christ, and looking to the coming together of all things in Christ – gives us an agenda far wider and deeper than either a crusading evangelism or what might unkindly be called a social gospel. Those who fail to preach Christ (but, remember, Christ crucified), and those who fail to see Christ in the poor, have both minimized the *Missio Dei*.

The second is our commitment to the Church. When in 2006 we extended our name to 'Anglicans in World Mission' we were aware how counter-cultural this could appear. Who, in this day and age, wants to identify with an inherited, institutional church? Fundamentalists who (although they pretend the opposite) are the products of modernism, and charismatic evangelicals who (although they cannot see it) are the children of post-modernism, prefer to choose their own loyalties. But USPG – and maybe it will be our undoing – works with the Church because we believe that it is an integral part of the *Missio Dei* and, for us, the Anglican Communion is a 'given'; literally our Communion is a gift from God. I've already spoken about the challenges of being post-colonial and coping with the plurality of contexts. So we have to try, in this post-Christendom era, to play our part in the Communion in the spirit of 'inter-dependence and mutual responsibility', and we need to recognize and respect the different and sometimes conflicting contexts in which our partners are seeking to engage in God's mission.

The third emphasis needs to be a dynamic spirituality, which can be difficult for a mission agency like ours which continues to have a funding role and where all the pressures of fund-raising are for the more attractive kind of development projects. So we need to return, as at the beginning of this chapter, to the Holy Trinity. Recent Anglican theology of church and mission has majored on the Trinity,[12] and although aware of the danger of over-structuralizing what we believe here[13] it does lead us to see ourselves as part of God's drawing-in and sending-out activity. In the end our assurance and the energy for our activity does not depend upon an institution or a book, but derives from the love of the Father, incorporating us in the Son, through the power of the Spirit.

I believe that the *Missio Dei* can help us avoid the pitfalls into which other agencies may have fallen. Mission must be about real and costly engagement with the world, embracing all that is meant by prophetic dialogue, but not to the extent where some Christian development agencies and many Christian charities play down the first and second Marks of Mission, concentrating on humanitarian work and justice issues, and ignoring both personal evangelism and the life of the Church. That seems very like the Pelagian heresy.

Equally, mission must be about acknowledging and proclaiming the centrality of Jesus Christ, but not to the extent of those who interpret the first Mark of Mission in such a way that the *Missio Dei* becomes a marketing and recruitment exercise where success will only be measured by individual conversion and church membership. That seems to me to be where the Gnostic heretics were heading.

God's activity in the world is larger and more challenging than all of these. And that's why we like to say in USPG that 'Mission is an adventure', God's adventure, which he calls us to join in.

An Anglican understanding of mission and evangelism

The theme of the 2008 Lambeth Conference was 'Equipping Bishops for Mission'. Among the resources which were prepared I was asked to suggest what might be distinctive in an Anglican approach to mission and evangelism.[14] I offered 12 points, making use of various reports which the Communion has commissioned:

1 The source and goal of all mission lies in the nature and work of the Trinity.
   'All our mission springs from the action and self-revelation of God in Jesus Christ . . . our call to mission and evangelism [is] grounded in the very nature of the God who is revealed to us.'[15]

2 All mission should be centred on Jesus Christ.
   'As Anglicans we are called to participate in God's mission in the world, by embracing respectful evangelism, loving service and prophetic witness. As we do so in all our varied contexts, we bear witness to and follow Jesus Christ, the crucified and risen Saviour.'[16]

3 Mission must be holistic, or 'integrated'.
   'As Anglicans, we value the "five marks of mission", which begin with the preaching of the Gospel and the call to personal conversion, but which embrace the whole of life: we would wish to see increased emphasis on ecumenism, peace-making and global mutuality as integral parts of God's mission. Mission is a rich and diverse pattern faithful to the proclamation of the Reign of God in Christ Jesus; a proclamation which touches all areas of life.'[17]

4 Understanding mission needs Scripture, tradition and reason.
   'Anglicans affirm the sovereign authority of the Holy Scriptures as the medium through which God by the Spirit communicates his work in the church and thus enables people to respond with understanding and faith', but also, *'Since the seventeenth century Anglicans have held that Scripture is to be understood and read in the light afforded by "tradition" and "reason".'*[18]

5 Theological diversity can be creative in understanding mission.

'As Anglicans we believe that both commonality and difference are sustained by apostolic truth and the hope of the final unity of all things as expressed in our worship . . . we need to look for, recognize, learn from and rejoice in the presence of Christ at work in the lives and situations of the other. This will lead to exploring differences and disagreements, and being willing to change in response to critique and challenge from others.' Above all we should 'live in the promise of God's reconciliation for ourselves and for the world'.[19]

6 The Church is an integral part of mission and its delivery.

'Because the Church as communion participates in God's communion of Father, Son and Holy Spirit, it has an eschatological reality and significance. The Church is the advent, in history, of God's final will being done "on earth as it is in heaven".'[20]

7 Mission must be rooted in the Incarnation of Christ.

'Confident in Christ, we join with all people of good will as we work for God's peace, justice and reconciling love. We recognize the immense challenges posed by secularization, poverty, unbridled greed, violence, religious persecution, environmental degradation, and HIV/Aids. In response, we engage in prophetic critique of destructive political and religious ideologies, and we build on a heritage of care for human welfare expressed through education, health care and reconciliation.'[21]

8 Mission must take its cultural context seriously.

'As Anglicans we are keenly aware that our common life and engagement in God's mission are tainted with shortcomings and failure, such as negative aspects of colonial heritage, self-serving abuse of power and privilege, undervaluing of the contributions of laity and women, inequitable distribution of resources, and blindness to the experience of the poor and oppressed. As a result, we seek to follow the Lord with renewed humility so that we may freely and joyfully spread the good news of salvation in word and deed.'[22]

9 In mission we continue to grow in our understanding of what God is doing.

'[Anglicanism is] not a system or a Confession but a method, a use, a direction' so that 'its greatest credentials are its incompleteness, with tension and travail in its soul. It is clumsy and untidy; it baffles neatness and logic. For it is sent not to commend itself as "the best type of Christianity", but by its very brokenness to point to the universal Church wherein all have died.'[23]

10 Mission is the responsibility of all the baptized under the leadership of the bishop.

'The primary task of every bishop, diocese and congregation in the Anglican Communion is to share in and show the love of God in Jesus Christ – by worship, by the proclamation to everyone of the gospel of salvation through Christ, through the announcing of good news to the poor and the continuing effort to witness to God's Kingdom and God's justice in act and word.'[24]

11 Mission should be a shared activity across the Communion.

'As the Communion continues to develop into a worldwide family of interdependent churches, we embrace challenges and opportunities for mission at local, regional, and international levels. In this, we cherish our faith and mission heritage as offering Anglicans distinctive opportunities for mission collaboration.'[25]

12 Mission should be part of a larger ecumenical giving and receiving.

'Our common mission is a mission shared with other churches and traditions beyond this covenant. We embrace opportunities for the discovery of the life of the whole gospel and for reconciliation and shared mission with the Church throughout the world. It is with all the saints that we will comprehend the fuller dimensions of Christ's redemptive and immeasurable love.'[26]

The Anglican way

This leads us finally to broaden out the consideration of Anglican perspectives from mission to the whole life and work of the Church – although if mission were to become the Church's central concern, as it should be, some of the other and more divisive issues might fall back into a more appropriate place! So where in our Anglican tradition can we look to recover some insights that may help us find a way through some of the current problems?

There has been no lack in recent years of those seeking to define the particular characteristics of Anglicanism, notably Stephen Sykes[27] and Paul Avis,[28] or in more popular form, Alastair Redfern.[29] Three recent writers have focused on how the received traditions of Anglicanism are to be found in the Communion's present state, and how they might help direct its future. It will be helpful to take some ideas from each of them.

Ian Douglas,[30] one of the key people in the design of the 2008 Lambeth Conference and now Bishop of Connecticut, defines Anglicanism as 'the embrace and celebration of apostolic catholicity within vernacular moments'. He shows how in the incarnation of Jesus, and in his ongoing body which is the Church, God acts in ways which are both particular and universal. Anglicanism has always rejoiced in its catholicity, as the Lambeth Quadrilateral shows, but it has also celebrated 'contextuality', from the English Reformation – and that particular historical context – to now. The missiologist Lamin Sanneh speaks of 'vernacular moments' when the gospel truth is translated and comes alive in a different place and culture. Anglicanism, says Douglas, should be ideally placed in the struggle to hold together the catholic and the local, the experienced and the received.

Bruce Kaye, until recently General Secretary of the Anglican Church in Australia, also sees Anglicanism as a story which over time and in each place – all very incarnational – has produced a particular catholicity in which the local and the universal are held together.[31] He traces how the inculturation which formed the Church of England, especially at the Reformation, took shape in many different cultural contexts around the world. He draws out both what is held in common, particularly in ministerial order and liturgy, and how the Anglican leaning towards conciliarity has inevitably reflected the different political realities in, say, the USA and Nigeria.

Kaye says that while Anglicanism's insistence on the historic episcopate makes it distinctive from other 'reformed' churches who may share the rest of the Lambeth Quadrilateral, it departs from the Roman model in understanding itself not as a church but as a fellowship of churches, in which the Province has increasingly been seen as the ecclesial unit and the place where local responsibility, not least for mission, is held together with catholic order. He points out that the Anglican Communion's Instruments of Unity are, unlike those of the Roman Catholic Church, fairly recent creations and (at least until the emergence of the proposed Covenant) without their jurisdictional character or aspirations.

One of his most helpful insights is in pointing out the contrast between the Doctrine Reports which the Communion has produced in recent years. 'For the Sake of the Kingdom', in 1987, was rooted in the actual empirical experiences of Anglican churches around the world, as it sought an extensive engagement with Scripture on the theme of creation and the kingdom of God. It thereby challenged all cultures, and could have led to a much more interdependent understanding of Church. However, by 1996 the Virginia Report, commissioned in the backlash caused by the US decision to ordain women, and working from what some see as a rather over-structural understanding of the Trinity, resulted in a much more uniform version of what it means to be Church and therefore how Anglicans should relate to each other.

Lorraine Cavanagh[32] takes as her starting point Richard Hooker's theology of 'participation' in understanding salvation and the life of the Church. Hooker saw the Church as participation in the life of God and within the dynamic of God's ongoing purpose. It is God who gives the Church its coherence and meaning. God's reconciliation of us with himself at a spiritual level is shown to the world by our desire to be reconciled with each other as 'a continual receiving of one another from within the love of God'.

She contrasts this with the more general trend in Reformation thought which saw moral values as autonomous virtues, apart from the spiritual character of holiness which reflects the justice and mercy of God. Then, as now, that trend led to a non-dynamic and divisive understanding of who God is and the kind of Church he wants.

It also led to relationships being based on purity rather than holiness. She says that the life and death of Jesus show how defining holiness on the basis of purity stifles compassion, creates division, causes backward-looking and non-dynamic Christian life, and generates fear and distrust.

It is this, she says, which underlies many of our present problems: 'Anglican disunity reveals the way in which non-dynamic thinking generates fixed beliefs in allowing doctrine and polity to become separated from the movement or dynamic of God's life in the Church as this proceeds from the dynamic of love within the Godhead.'

Her answer is that we need to rediscover Anglican hospitality – 'receiving one another unconditionally from within a shared love of God' – as expressed in the Eucharist, and the way we work together to find truth in Scripture. When we do this we reflect thereby that hospitality of God which marks all salvation history. We need to honour each other's integrity because we trust in God and our covenantal relationship with him.

Who could disagree that if we could find a way to live out together this 'hospitality of Christ crucified', what a different Communion we would be!

5

The Church in mission today

The Church and mission

Mission is the activity of God in the world. It's what God is doing, but more than that, it's the overflowing into this world of who God is: if the heart of God (as formulated in the doctrine of the Trinity) is loving relationship, giving and receiving, sending and surrendering, in fact the *koinonia* which we translate as Communion, then mission is the expression of this from Creation onwards, through the Christ event, in the sending of the Spirit, so that 'Christ shall be all in all'.[1]

So it is God who has the mission, not the Church, and if one may think spatially for a moment this activity of God is two-way. In one direction, the Church is part of God's mission, brought into being through Christ to become his Body in the world, and to be sent out by the Spirit and with the Spirit into the world to serve God's kingdom. In the other direction, as the Virginia Report puts it, those who are made 'brothers and sisters in Christ' through baptism are 'embraced in the communion of God the Holy Trinity'.[2] This finds expression in both Eucharist and mission:

> United to Christ, each member of the Body relates to the other members; they are interdependent with and through Christ. To celebrate the eucharist together reveals and builds this mutuality. 'We who are many are one body for we all partake of the one bread.' In eucharist the Spirit affirms and renews communion in Christ and the gifts given us to participate in the divine mission.[3]

There are, according to the Nicene Creed, four marks of the Church. We are to be One, to show the world the unity which comes from knowing that the beginning and end of all things is in Christ. We are to be Holy, set apart and distinctive, not to glory in our own self-righteousness, but to demonstrate a way of life quite different from the usual ways of the world. We are to be Catholic, holding together the past and the present, but also the diversity which comes from following Christ in so many different places and cultures. And we are to be Apostolic.

This apostolic nature of the Church arises directly from our being sent into the world, just as Christ came into the world and as the Holy Spirit sent the first followers of Christ out into the world. The calling of the Church in each place and in every generation is to be the Body of Christ, and to respond to the leading of the Spirit, in the particular context – geographical, social, cultural – in which it finds itself. The phrase 'into the world' has its dangers: it can suggest too hard and fast a separation of Church and world, and it must not blind us to the fact that the Church, as part of the world, is also subject to failure and capable of being mistaken. But it reminds us that in the end the Church exists not for its own sake, but for the sake of the world for which Christ died.

Mission around the Anglican Communion

Let me illustrate this mission with some snapshots from around the Anglican Communion today. From the years since its founding in 1701, USPG has found itself in historic relationship with 28 of the Communion's member churches. What follows are only single examples of what mission means for some of those churches, but put together these stories also form a broad tapestry of the Five Marks of Mission in action. All of them have benefited from direct or indirect USPG support.

Argentina

The Anglican Church in Argentina is in a process of transformation, working to integrate Spanish- and English-speaking congregations. This has enabled it to grow and reach more people. As a consequence, priests need to be trained, equipped, prepared and supported in their roles. The Revd Michael Wilkie, a teacher and priest from the Church of England, has been working in the Diocese of Argentina to write and set up training courses for lay and ordained people.

Bangladesh

Water poisoning with naturally occurring arsenic has put almost 40 million people in Bangladesh at risk of illnesses that can lead to cancer. The Church of Bangladesh has a programme to dig new wells so that villagers have access to clean water. Technical advice is provided by an English development worker supported by a number of Church of England agencies.

Brazil

In one of the favelas (slums) around the new capital of Brasilia, the nearby parish priest celebrates a weekly Eucharist and chairs the protest movement for sanitation and running water. Meanwhile in Amazonia, the bishop of the new missionary diocese is standing up for the rights of indigenous people, putting himself at grave personal risk.

The Caribbean

Trinidad and Tobago is a developing nation facing rising crime rates, particularly among young people. The Anglican Church here has a unique opportunity to reach out to children through its primary schools, using music to improve self-esteem and all-round development. Through music, the project aims to draw children more fully into the life of the school, the church and the wider community.

Ethiopia

USPG Mission Companions Andrew and Janice Proud have been based at St Matthew's Church, in Addis Ababa, since 2002. Andrew serves as Area Bishop of Ethiopia and the Horn of Africa and he and Janice are working with the church's outreach programmes. Some of the churches he oversees are in the Gambella region that borders Sudan, including churches set up to provide help and encouragement for Sudanese refugees who fled civil war in their home country.

Ghana

The seminary of St Nicholas in Cape Coast trains new priests and is a centre for African theology. Elsewhere the Church runs rural health clinics and orphanages for children in a country where infant mortality is high due to malaria and a lack of clean water.

India

India has an estimated 18 million street children, and in the capital city the Delhi Brotherhood, part of the Church of North India, provides a safe home and education for those who would otherwise be exploited and abused.

The Indian Ocean

In Madagascar many families struggle to feed their children, let alone send them to school. For orphaned or disabled children, life is even harder. The Church is running hostels where accommodation, school fees, books and pencils, uniforms and medical care are all provided.

Israel-Palestine

The small but faithful Anglican Church centred in Jerusalem is primarily Palestinian, defending the rights of people on the West Bank, but wanting to work with all those, Arab and Israeli, who are committed to justice and reconciliation. It also runs a hospital in Nablus caring for people on all sides.

Japan

Life is hard for children from Japan's Filipino community, both economically and socially; with no legal status, access to education is limited. Many have been born in Japan to Filipina mothers. The Church is working among these children providing them with an education, including lessons in Filipino culture.

Korea

Towards Peace in Korea (TOPIK) is a project run by the Anglican Church of Korea. It teaches about peace and works for reconciliation, as part of the church's support for the reunification of North and South Korea.

Malawi

In one of the poorest countries in the world many people still rely on the churches for the most basic health care provision. An English doctor and USPG Mission Companion works in two large and under-resourced hospitals as well as in eight health centres over 160 miles apart.

Malaysia

In this overwhelmingly Muslim country the Anglican Church, founded in Kuching in 1856, is part, with Singapore, of a Province where the commitment to evangelism is bearing fruit in growing churches and an increasing number of young people being attracted to the Christian faith.

Mozambique

The Anglican Church played a prominent part in the peace-making here after many years of civil war following independence, literally turning 'guns into ploughshares'.

Myanmar

Despite all the challenges of living under a long-established military regime, the Church here continues its faithful witness and social care programmes. It was among the first to respond when Cyclone Nargis devastated the south of the country in 2008.

Pakistan

This United Church, despite its minority status, works for peace on the border with Afghanistan, and in Lahore has pioneered attempts at Christian–Muslim dialogue. It also runs health programmes for young women.

Peru

An increasing number of missions in places like the northern slums of Lima are growing in size through their combination of eucharistic worship, evangelism, and social action with the poor.

The Philippines

The two Anglican churches here, one established by the Americans and the other originating from independence movements, are both involved in campaigns for social justice, especially against the inroads of foreign mining companies.

Polynesia

The Church here increasingly sees its mission as combating climate change and the effects already being experienced in its low-lying islands.

Southern Africa

In addition to its pivotal role in post-apartheid 'justice and reconciliation' work, the Church is deeply involved in caring for the victims, and especially the orphans, of HIV/AIDS.

Sri Lanka

The Church was in the forefront of caring for people after the 2004 tsunami, and following the Sinhalese military victory over the Tamils in 2009 continues to work with Buddhist monks to seek reconciliation between Tamils and Sinhalese.

Tanzania

Training of new priests continues in the old UMCA theological college in Dar-es-Salaam, and the Anglican Church has now created its own university in the new capital of Dodoma.

Zambia

In addition to its long-established work providing healthcare in remote regions, the Church in Zambia is now combating the spread of malaria through the 'Nets for Life' programme.

Zimbabwe

Despite suffering from political machinations and the economic hardships resulting from the actions of the present government, the Church here continues to be active in feeding programmes and other care, especially for children, supported by the (Church of England) Archbishops' Zimbabwe Appeal, administered by USPG.

The above are just glimpses of how churches around the Communion are engaged in God's work. They are autonomous churches, and the mission belongs to them. The priorities are for them to decide, not the mission agencies which may have founded them nor the donors from more affluent countries who may decide to support them. But as the rest of this chapter will show, colonialism, past and present, plays an important part in what they decide to do, and where they can find the resources to do it.

Before moving on, we should note one other aspect of the Church's mission which is challenging colonialism. Countries like Canada and Australia may have established an identity apart from Britain and the Church of England, but they are still dealing with the colonial inheritance as it affects, or more sadly rejects, their own indigenous peoples. Perhaps New Zealand has done most in addressing these issues: the Anglican Church in Aotearoa, New Zealand and Polynesia holds together the 'Pakeha' (European), Maori and Pacific peoples and cultures, led by three co-presiding archbishops, one from each constituency.

Changing relationships

During the colonial period, 'mission' meant taking the gospel from the North to the South, and planting the Church in other parts of the world. We have seen how different churches and their mission agencies, European and North American, undertook this task, until the realization – particularly since the Anglican Congress in Toronto in 1963 – that it should be a more mutual and multi-directional process. This was partly because the receiving parties were now churches, and often strongly growing churches, in their own right, but also because the more colonial understandings of mission became deeply suspect.

The Anglican Consultative Council put it like this in 1973:

> The responsibility for mission in any place belongs primarily to the church in that place. However, the universality of the Gospel and the oneness of God's mission also mean that this mission must be shared in each and every place with fellow Christians from each and every part of the world with their distinctive insights and contributions...

The oneness of the missionary task must make us all givers and receivers.[4]

Two more recent developments have been the emergence of mission agencies within what was once a receiving country – such as the Indian Missionary Society, founded in 1903 to evangelize within India itself and now with over 500 full-time missionaries[5] – and the unfortunately named 'Reverse Mission'. The latter comprises missionaries coming from the South to the North, either within a programme of genuine interchange, or because they believe that Europe needs to be reconverted to Christianity – the reversal of what happened during the colonial era. However, the majority of missionaries today are still from the North, and most of these are from North America.[6]

Another aspect of the reversal process is the church-planting that has resulted from migration: the leadership of the largest single churches in Britain (the Kingsway International Christian Centre in East London) and in the Ukraine (the Embassy of the Blessed Kingdom of God for All Nations in Kiev) is Nigerian. The 'mainstream' churches in the UK have also benefited from such immigration: my previous parish in Blackbird Leys, Oxford, would be a struggling housing estate church were it not for the presence of a lively Afro-Caribbean membership, and many inner-city parishes in the Diocese of Southwark where I now serve have found new life thanks to Anglicans from West Africa.

Patterns of support

Although first emphasized at the Whitby, Ontario meeting of the International Missionary Council in 1947, the word which truly emerged from the 1960s onwards in the rethinking of old colonial patterns of mission support was 'partnership'. Ideally it meant that churches now realized that they were engaged in a common task – God's global mission – and were called to support each other in it. Its use recognized that in this new relationship each had riches to share. There was the North's economic advantage, although the decline in European (but not US) church-going would soon weaken this, as did the withdrawal of the church tax in Germany and elsewhere. And there was the South's spiritual vitality, although this could be easily over-romanticized.

However, the economic imbalance, especially between North America and the countries of the South, meant that real partnership often gave way to new forms of dependency, or indeed colonialism. In 1989 the WCC Conference on World Mission and Evangelism made a renewed call for 'common decision-making structures and ensuring reciprocal sharing in mission . . . as part of, and as a sign of, God's intention that all should share in the one *oikoumene*'. It spoke out against the paternalism which 'both consolidates the power of the rich and discourages the people of the South from doing what they are quite able to do'.[7]

The 1999 report from Missio,[8] the Anglican Communion's Standing Commission on Mission, suggested that the very word 'partner' sounded too much like a business relationship, and advocated instead 'companions' – literally, those who eat bread together. Language is important, and it's particularly sad how in the Episcopal Church both conservatives and liberals still talk of 'sending missionaries', 'taking the gospel to Africa', and – because being sure where your money is being spent is so much part of the deal – themselves 'going on mission', as if two weeks doing some community activity in a developing country is about genuine engagement rather than meeting their own needs.

European agencies have tried to be more careful. CMS replaced the word 'missionary' with 'mission partner', while for USPG it is the receiving church which is the partner, so personnel are now called 'Mission Companions'. More fundamentally, these agencies have sought to reorganize themselves in response to the post-colonial realities. CMS has 'regionalized' and now has offices in Ghana, Kenya and South Korea as well as in Oxford in the UK. CMS Africa now exists in its own right, and a CMS-Latin America may result from the organization's 2009 merger with the South America Missionary Society (SAMS). These developments, part of the Anglican Communion but standing alongside rather than within the existing church structures, are a further sign of the ecclesiology which we have already noted in the history of CMS.

USPG, with its rather different ecclesiology, has not gone down that route, having always claimed to be 'the handmaid of the Church' rather than pursuing its own identity and agenda. Its response to the need to find an appropriate post-colonial role has been to open up policy-making and budget-setting to international consultation, so partner Provinces can see themselves as 'heirs together' of the colonial history and equal partners in the current work.

However, while at least some mission agencies have tried to address the colonial inheritance, other developments have risked its reinvention. One of the results of the Toronto Congress was the exercise known as 'Partners-in-Mission', in which each church worked on its mission priorities and then shared them with visitors from other parts of the Communion. This led to the setting up of companion links between dioceses, usually one from the North and one from the South. At first the policy, at least in the Church of England, was that these partnerships were for prayer and mutual support, but increasingly they became channels for funding, bypassing the mission agencies.

Today these companion links dominate the relationships within the Communion. In North America they are heavily funded by the dioceses concerned. At best they provide real meeting-places for people, including bishops, to get to know each other, participate in each other's life, and in some places engage in frank discussion of the problems besetting the wider Communion. At worst they are channels for sending money without proper safeguards, or for the funding of cherry-picked projects which are more about the richer companion's wishes than the need of the partner diocese for support in its ongoing work.

Underlying such developments has been a significant change in Western culture, especially among those who give money for what they may still call 'overseas mission'. There was a time when, however paternalistic the motives, the colonial relationship gave rise to a sense of obligation. Church of England parishes, for example, would set aside a sum of money, even a percentage of their annual income, for 'missions'. Indeed for a long time mission agencies felt no obligation to say where the money went – they, on behalf of the Church, would decide! Today Christians as much as any other charitably inclined people are part of a donor culture in which those who give want to decide where their (sic) money goes. We are back here to those 'post-modern' questions about how inherited senses of belonging and commitment have been replaced by consumerism and self-selection.

Mission agencies, like other charities, have had to respond by offering the kind of projects which donors, both individuals and churches, will find attractive. At best this is still work which partners have nominated from their own mission priorities, but the temptation is to go for the softer, some might say 'sexier', projects which donors prefer rather than those which partners prioritize. It's also true, at a time when established programmes of sending people overseas might be better replaced by supporting and training personnel from within the partner church, or from a nearby Province, that donors much prefer to have missionaries who can report back first hand on where their money has gone.

But even this may not be enough. The move to choose and own what you support is leading local churches and even individuals to set up their own charities, send their own missionaries and bypass mission agencies altogether. The result is an increasingly inequitable pattern of relationships across the Communion. There was already a problem here with companion links, where some dioceses in the South, and frequently those with more entrepreneurial bishops, were benefiting from support which other, often poorer dioceses were unable to access. This makes it even worse.

Obviously in all of this I have an axe to grind, as General Secretary of USPG, but like many of the other mission agencies in the UK we believe that our holistic understanding of God's mission, and our commitment to the Communion as a whole, remain crucial for its future. Our 'heirs together' process is about making these decisions with all the partners involved. In addition to our continuing support for all that they do, and especially in healthcare, we have recently reaffirmed the priority of training leaders, both ordained and lay: this is not the easiest thing for which to raise money, even from church congregations, but it's vital for our partners all around the Communion that they can discern those who will be their future leaders and train them for what they will need as bishops, clergy, teachers, development officers, or whatever.

What is certainly true is that a renewed emphasis on mission would be a welcome relief to the other – many would say, secondary – issues which currently take up the Communion's time and energy. Indeed, it would put some of those other issues in perspective. 'Communion is ... primarily based upon relationships of mutual responsibility and interdependence in the body of Christ across the differences of culture, location, ethnicity, and even theological perspective to serve God's mission in the world,' says Bishop Ian Douglas: 'Common efforts to serve God's mission of reconciliation and restoration across differences offer glimpses into the possibilities for the unity and future of the Anglican Communion.'[9]

Mission and development

There is another reason why mission agencies face an increasingly challenging future. During the colonial era missionaries were not just evangelists and church-planters, they were often the only providers of education and healthcare. In large parts of Africa and India today the church-run schools and hospitals continue to play a significant role. Many of the first African nationalist leaders came from church schools, and even today leading families from other faith communities in places like Pakistan and Sri Lanka send their children to them.

In the middle of the last century other organizations came on to the scene. Some have grown into the national and transnational development agencies now known as NGOs (non-governmental organizations). At the same time Western governments had to ask themselves how far they should continue to provide economic support to colonies achieving political independence – an issue not separate, of course, from the question as to how they could continue to profit from these new nation states. UK churches have played their part, not least in the partly successful campaigns to cancel the international debt which has been a dead hand on emerging economies – the so-called Highly Indebted Poor Countries – since the oil boom of the 1970s, and in the attempt to raise overseas aid to 0.7 per cent of GNP.

It's sad that partner churches around the world experience a certain ambivalence when trying to access funding from bodies like the UK's Department of Overseas Development: many Western governments, and especially that of the UK, have a secularist agenda which makes them suspicious of 'faith' and fearful of religious proselytism. This Western agenda, together with the continued exploitation of developing economies and the inequity in international trade, is seen by commentators in the South as the reinvention of colonialism, seeking to impose Western values while taking economic advantage. However, Western governments and NGOs, especially in their newly found commitment to grass-roots development, can't escape the fact that on the ground it is often faith-based communities who have the values and systems which can deliver. The World Health Organization estimates that between 30 and 70 per cent of healthcare in Africa is provided by faith-based organizations.

Where in all of this do the Christian development agencies fit? Since they began to emerge after the Second World War they have taken over many of the education and healthcare interests of the mission agencies, and easily eclipse them in seeking money for this work from church people in Britain and Ireland.[10] But there are some important theological issues here, about mission and about their relationship with the Church.

The Roman Catholic organization CAFOD, and Tearfund which came from the evangelical churches, both embrace an understanding of mission which they describe as 'holistic' or 'integral', because they would see their particular concern for social and economic development as part of the larger *Missio Dei*. Historically, CAFOD is grounded in Catholic social teaching such as Pope Paul VI's *Populorum progressio*,[11] while Tearfund appeals to the kind of theology set out in the Lausanne Covenant of 1974, which asserts that 'evangelism and socio-political involvement are both part of our Christian duty'.[12] Christian Aid, on the other hand, has been more shaped by the kind of post-colonial and secular theology which emerged in the World Council of Churches from the 1960s, in which 'the world sets the agenda'.[13] One outcome of this theology was that mission became very much identified with poverty reduction, human rights and, more recently, climate change, while proclaiming the gospel, especially when among people of other faiths, became less acceptable.

For the same reasons Christian Aid also holds a different understanding of 'church'. Its sponsors are the Anglican and Free Churches, in the same way that CAFOD is the official agency of the Roman Catholic Church, but unlike CAFOD and Tearfund, who work mainly through the churches in developing countries, Christian Aid chooses its partners much more widely. Sometimes they are ecumenical organizations, and sometimes they have nothing to do with the Church. Rarely will they be Anglican dioceses. The reason given is a practical one, that the churches are often not the most effective partners, but the practice also reveals a missiology and ecclesiology at variance with current thinking on the *Missio Dei*. In the USA, the Episcopal Church's Episcopal Relief and Development (ERD) manages to be a highly regarded international aid and develop-ment agency while still giving priority to its Anglican Communion partners in delivering its work. As a result of the 2008 Lambeth Conference, there is now a proposal for an alliance of Anglican relief and development agencies, Global Anglican Relief and Development Alliance (GARDA), to improve co-ordination in development, relief and advocacy work across the Communion. Meanwhile the more conservative Provinces have tried to distance themselves from the Episcopal Church and ERD by setting up an alternative 'Anglican Relief and Development Fund'.

Where does this leave mission agencies like USPG today? There are those who believe that the emergence of more direct relationships, such as Diocesan Links, allied to the trends in donor culture to want to know and in some sense 'sponsor' what you are funding, means the end of generic agencies. Some will argue the same from the stance of development agencies that would reduce the mission agenda to social concerns, and doubt whether evangelism has any place in a globalized, multi-faith world. Others will side with that part of the world church which fits their own, more conservative theology, and only want to maintain those relationships. Surely the *Missio Dei* is larger than any of these?

6

Globalization and the post-colonial Church

————•◆•————

I said at the beginning of this book that our history and theology need to be seen through the lenses of post-modernism, post-imperialism and post-colonialism. These concepts are complex and disputed, and they reinforce each other. They have sometimes been used to discredit religious faith and experience, but they can also enable us to see more clearly some of the difficulties which we face. When discussing mission and communion they can present challenging questions to holistic ways of thinking and to relationships based on inherited loyalties.

Post-modernism – the way we think

Some post-modern approaches to knowledge lead to nihilism, because they so deconstruct language and reduce reality that there is little left which can be said, let alone believed as having ultimate value. They leave us with a universe which has no meaning whatsoever. But, as often pointed out, this is itself a 'meta-narrative', the kind of overriding interpretation which the proponents of post-modernism have claimed can no longer exist.

There are, however, some aspects of this approach to truth which can lead us into greater truth. One is the freedom not to be shackled by the limitations of modernity, but to be able to revisit what was believed before: the Enlightenment's emphasis on rationalism and rights brought great advances and freedoms, but its individualism and instrumentalism also reduced our responsibilities for each other and for creation, and limited our sense of wonder and of faith.

An important aspect of post-modernist thought for this present study is the attention it gives to what is called 'discourse'. The post-modern theorist Michel Foucault[1] described how concepts and principles coalesce into coherent systems of thought, so shaping and limiting how people think and act. The obvious example in our present study is the colonial belief in the moral and cultural superiority of the West and the resulting assumption that the rest of the world was uncivilized. This legitimized the subjugation of alien peoples, and then gave rise to colonial education systems based on a Western intellectualism which assumed it had nothing to learn from the cultures which were the discourses of the local people.

Revisiting our history in this way encourages us to look again at what we take for granted, such as how we do theology and how we make ethical decisions about what is right and what is wrong. It makes us more aware of our identity – how we belong to a particular national, cultural or confessional grouping – and how we react to those who belong to different groupings. Most important, it asks us who has determined these frameworks of understanding: the question, again, about where the power lies. Who decided in the past, and who decides now, what is right and true, what the Church should teach and where boundaries are to be set?

This takes us to another of the post-modern theorists, Jacques Derrida, and his work on 'deconstruction'.[2] Derrida said that the over-objective understanding of the world which came with the Enlightenment led to the conceptual binary oppositions which make up the structure of Western thought: man/woman, Western/Eastern, mind/body, public/private. Derrida suggests that these are hierarchically structured, with one term in each pair being privileged over the other. This is the kind of analysis which has allowed some liberation theology to develop a theology and spirituality in which those who have up to now been rendered powerless can find a voice. We have also seen how in some 'inclusivist' theologies the same kind of analysis might lead to a surrender to mere subjectivism. Rather, as Richard Rohr puts it, it is an invitation to dialogue with 'the other', whether that's God or people who are different from us.[3]

I began this book by discussing how the Anglican Communion emerged from the European and US missionary movements during colonial times, and I have suggested that in our post-colonial period a major division exists between those who call themselves traditionalists – often claiming to go back to a pre-modern culture but in many ways the product of a later modernism – and those who are accused of going beyond both pre-modernism and modernism, and embracing post-modern thought to the extent of advocating a different religion.

Put another way, we are experiencing the interplay of three different cultural outlooks. That is not to say that any culture is a static thing – the very nature of culture is another of the hotly contested concepts in the understanding of how different groups structure their reality – but it may help us to see how the various 'discourses' one hears around the Anglican Communion have emerged.

First, there is the 'pre-modern'. It's the world in which the events in the Bible took place – a pre-scientific age when gods existed and intervened on earth, where myths and miracles went unquestioned. It is where much traditional African religion still finds its home, which is why African Christians immediately recognize their world in Scripture. It is where the Ghanaian theologian John Pobee locates much African theology: the African Christ claims and redeems the whole of life, leading to holistic mission, and to the rejection of the intellectual division between body and spirit brought by the Western missionaries.[4]

Similarly, the Nigerian Jesuit priest Agbonkhianmeghe Orobator draws on Chinua Achebe's novel *Things Fall Apart* to show the often hostile encounter between such traditional religious beliefs and practices and the first Christian missionaries. He contrasts the hard and often exclusive theology which came from Europe with the warmth of the real gospel of grace, the more narrative style of African culture, and the African emphasis on community both with the ancestors and among the people now.[5] (The pre-modern is also, strangely, the world of Harry Potter, which says something good or bad, and probably both, about our wish to escape back to it.)

The pre-modern world is often thought to be hierarchical, and usually patriarchal, although some Africans say that the political despotism – and monarchical episcopacy! – which they sometimes experience today draws from colonial patterns of power rather than from the more consensual style which characterized tribal headship. It is nevertheless true that in a pre-modern culture communal stability and security come before individual fulfilment.

Second, there is the 'modernism' which came with the Enlightenment and which – despite the attempt of some mission movements to escape its challenges by taking a simpler faith abroad – was actually what was exported during the colonial era. It still determines how most people in Europe, North America and increasingly Asia see their world. It can weaken religion, but, as we have noted with Anglican traditionalists – and there are fundamentalist movements in other religions which display the same characteristics[6] – it can result in faith systems where previously 'mythological' concepts and texts are now treated empirically. Another example would be the 'prosperity gospel' where faith becomes a lever into the economic system.

Third, there is the very fluid area of 'post-modernism'. The US church historian Martin Marty describes what has happened to Western culture as a major shift from the centripetal drive towards unity evident at the middle of the last century to the operation of centrifugal forces in many areas of life by its end. He speaks of a decisive historical change towards the particularized, the centrifugal, in politics, culture and religion.[7] I saw this tendency at first hand during my ten years as Bishop of Swindon, in a growing, high-tech and very mobile new city where few people inherited any sense of belonging to a place, a community, a political party or a church. It can lead to psychological and cultural homelessness. Employment was insecure or intense, often short-term and serial, and relationships including marriage could follow the same pattern. At work people were part of a global economy, but home could mean just the television, computer and designer drugs for the weekend.

Traditional institutions do not flourish in this globalized but privatized culture. Writing about pastoral theology, John Reader talks about the 'zombie categories', the activities and beliefs that once made sense of the world; these have not passed away altogether, but they no longer resonate with the way people live and think, and can no longer provide meaning for their lives.[8] Where does public worship, or even moral teaching, fit into this world?

On the positive side, such post-modernity allows the freedom of self-expression and the opportunity to unmask the kinds of injustice and abuse of power found in inherited systems. But it also risks taking everything away except the subjective feelings of the individual consumer. Church-wise, this can be seen in some aspects of both charismatic evangelicalism and those who have embraced the inclusivity agenda in North America. In describing revivalism, Martyn Percy points out that the language used in the age of nineteenth-century imperialism was military and monarchical, whereas today it's more likely to be intimate and erotic.[9] Although declaring very different theologies, it would seem that both conservatives and liberals can reflect this culture, one which is ultimately dependent on feelings as much as on facts.

Post-imperialism – and a new globalization

We have seen how the Anglican Communion came into being as the result of the British, and to a lesser extent the US Empire. During the years since Britain lost or gave up its empire we have experienced two competing empires in the Cold War, and now only the USA may be said to exercise such imperial influence. China is the growing economic force, but how far it will seek political power in the future remains to be seen.

However, imperialism lives on. It has acquired new forms and powers through globalization, which has been described as the 'trans-national flows of capital, people, commodities, images and/or ideologies',[10] something which is happening with increasing speed and density, and which is increasingly done remotely rather than through contact between people.

The result has been that, despite having achieved political independence, many countries are still 'colonial' because they remain dependent on Western-based global economic systems. Even Western nation-states can now feel like colonies whose powers have been taken over by global corporations and financial flows over which they have little control.

It's not only economic. Opening the 2009 Synod of Roman Catholic bishops, which concerned itself with Africa, Pope Benedict denounced how the West's materialism and lack of moral values were being spread around the world. 'There is absolutely no doubt that the so-called "First" World has exported up to now and continues to export its spiritual toxic waste that contaminates the peoples of other continents, particularly those of Africa,' he said. 'In this sense colonialism, which is over at a political level, has never really entirely come to an end.'[11]

Globalization has created the technological means whereby members of a world Church can relate to each other as never before, but this ease of communication and organization has also been one of the contributors to Anglican disunity as those who are unhappy with developments elsewhere in the Communion have found it more possible to gather and lobby – depending, of course, on who has the opportunity and funding to access the resources!

Globalization has also made us more aware of Christianity as a 'world religion'. There are well over two billion Christians in the world today, and by 2050 they will make up 34 per cent of the world's population: there will be about three Christians for every two Muslims worldwide.[12] It is often said in current Anglican Communion disputes that it is the church in the South which is growing, displacing Europe as the principal centre of Christianity. This is certainly true in Africa, although it must be pointed out that it is religion in general which is growing: globally Islam may be growing faster than Christianity, although in both cases birth rate may be a larger factor than conversions.

Commentators like Philip Jenkins speak of this global shift as the inexorable growth of a 'new Christendom'. He suggests that by 2050, six countries (Brazil, Mexico, the Philippines, Nigeria, Congo and the USA) will each have at least 100 million Christians, while Brazil itself will have at least 150 million Catholics and 40 million Protestants. The number of Pentecostalists will exceed one billion.

The reality underneath the statistics may need more teasing out. Church leaders in, for example, sub-Saharan Africa have themselves asked questions, especially after the Rwanda massacres,[13] about the depth of Christian conviction in situations where missionaries 'converted' communities rather than individuals, and when desperately poor people are attracted to schools and hospitals, let alone to the claims of the prosperity gospel. Miranda Hassett records similar concerns about nominal Christians among Ugandan Anglicans.[14]

Such leaders also wonder about the future. If no part of the world is to be spared the intrusions of globalization, what kind of Christianity will the next generation need? It is often assumed in Europe that modernization means secularization, and therefore calls for a more liberal Church, but that is not necessarily the case in the USA, and certainly not in the global South where it is the US conservative missions who are currently making the running, with the assistance of all the opportunities offered by globalism and especially through tele-evangelism.

So these growing churches are by and large conservative:

> The types of Christianity that have thrived most successfully in the global South have been very different from what many Europeans and North Americans consider mainstream. These models have been far more enthusiastic, much more centrally concerned with the immediate workings of the supernatural, through prophecy, visions, ecstatic utterances, and healing.[15]

Some see this as a new outpouring of the Holy Spirit. Others ask whether it is more to do with enthusiastic Africans (for instance) essentially reviving the pagan practices of their traditional societies.

At one level religious conservatism is a reaction against globalization, and especially against the secularizing tendencies of its economic systems. There is a clear contrast between ideologies which commodify and those which sacramentalize, or in the more popular phrase, it can be 'McWorld vs Jihad'. However, conservatives in the Church may not be quite as anti-globalist as they first appear. Here we touch again on the question about whether quasi-fundamentalist movements are more a reflection of modernism than of the pre-modernism they claim. More practically, if globalization is less about institutions and histories, and more about building networks, using technology and crossing cultures or creating universal cultures, then the alternative structures which are now emerging in the Anglican Communion are taking full advantage of it.[16]

Postcolonialism – the power we wield

Post-colonialism (with a hyphen) refers to the period after, for example, the achievement of independence by African nation-states. It is helpful to distinguish this from postcolonialism (unhyphenated), a much more involved process to do with the way in which such countries are emerging, insofar as they can, from identities which were shaped by the imperial powers. Very often the peoples of colonized lands were seen as inferior and uncivilized, racial differences were institutionalized, and so colonial and imperial rule could be legitimized. In his introduction to the subject, Robert J. C. Young says that postcolonialism is about turning the world upside down. 'It means realizing that when western people look at the non-western world what they see is often more of a mirror image of themselves and their own assumptions than the reality of what is really there, or of how people outside the west actually feel and perceive themselves.'[17]

We can begin unpacking this term by looking at two of its early exponents. Edward Said was a Palestinian, a member of a people who still today are defined by others and unable to chart their own future. In his classic book *Orientalism* he drew attention to the exercise of power:

> What I am interested in doing now is suggesting how the general liberal consensus that 'true' knowledge is fundamentally non-political (and conversely, that overtly political knowledge is not 'true' knowledge) obscures the highly if obscurely political circumstances obtaining when knowledge is produced. No one is helped in understanding this today when the adjective 'political' is used as a label to discredit any work for daring to violate the protocol of pretended suprapolitical objectivity.[18]

Frantz Fanon was born in the French colony of Martinique in the Caribbean, but it was as a psychiatrist in Algeria that he began first to see that what his patients most needed was release from passive victimhood into a status as subjects who could determine their own futures, and then to apply that to the way the whole colonial system imprisoned and dehumanized people by claiming the right to label and thereby restrict them. 'Because it is a systematic negation of the other person and a furious determination to deny the other person all attributes of humanity, colonialism forces the people to ask themselves the question constantly: "In reality, who am I?"[19]

So colonialism is not just about political and military domination but also about cultural hegemony, and how those in power assert this superiority and their right to represent the other. In the nineteenth century, in the rise of what is sometimes called social Darwinism, the aspect of race came to play a large part in the kind of anthropological theories which could justify other forms of exploitation. Race continues today to feature, consciously and unconsciously, in how we value or devalue people who are different from us or who have a different view of the world.

The Church in a post-everything world

I've been suggesting that the *Missio Dei* should properly be seen as the dynamic activity of God in the world – sending, freeing, serving, relating – reflecting the very nature of God himself (or herself, or themselves). Historically, and going back at least to Constantine, mission has been more a matter of dissemination and control. Although both theory and practice wavered, that was often the case through the colonial years of the modern missionary movements. Such power systems no longer hold sway. Indeed, we may rejoice that the powers which operated in such systems have been dethroned.

So how far can the Christian gospel still be seen as something which is received and passed on? Some would say that such 'meta-narratives' are a thing of the past: there can no longer be 'essentials' which are true for all time and in all places, and which merely need to be applied in each different time and place. One might ask, in passing, what has taken their place? Do the powers of globalization offer anything better, for those who benefit from them, let alone for those who are subject to them? Has the global marketplace actually generated just another meta-narrative, one in which human existence (and the created order) is measured in commodities, and human beings are reduced to mere consumers?

What we can say is that such thinking alerts us to the exercise of power in mission, the use and abuse of power when the gospel is preached and the Church seeks to grow. Kortright Davis, an Anglican priest originally from Antigua in the West Indies, sees the colonial era as imposing a 'culture of dominance' – military, political, economic – which

> manifested itself in much of the missionary activity of the century, where in the name of God and the gospel, peoples have been robbed of their cultural heritage, assaulted by a foreign spirit, and torn asunder in their souls by the lure of material gain wrapped up in pious fantasy. For to control people's fears and people's faith is to exercise a reign of dominance that is hard to overcome.[20]

This is what happens when the *Missio Dei* is about selling a particular religion or extending someone's own type of church, as in our own day when evangelism is reduced to marketing and recruitment. Perhaps the modern missionary movements did see themselves as a continuation of the 'light to lighten the Gentiles', going out from Europe or America just as the first missionaries had gone out from Jerusalem, but if so they failed to understand what actually happened during those first years of the Christian Church.

In his seminal work on the missionary movement in Christian history, which he subtitles *Studies in the Transmission of Faith*, Andrew Walls argues that from the Council of Jerusalem onwards the Church was a pilgrim people seeking to indigenize the gospel according to the particulars of each culture and group. That was why Paul opposed the Jewish insistence on the retention of their food laws and the Greeks who pretended they were Jews by being circumcised. Conversion was to be about transformation rather than substitution. For Walls that means, 'No group of Christians has therefore any right to impose in the name of Christ upon another group of Christians a set of assumptions about life determined by another time and place.'[21] So he celebrates the message of Ephesians: it's 'as if the very diversity of Christian humanity makes it complete'.

Our problem is knowing where such diversity has its limits, and so what criteria there may be for evaluating the way in which the gospel becomes part of any particular culture. Essential to the New Testament's understanding of such things is the presence of the Holy

Spirit. The missiologist Christopher Duraisingh suggests that Pentecost was 'letting the Gospel loose', after which tradition, including 'The Apostolic Tradition', can only be dynamic, a matter of handing over rather than handing on, a relational process which belongs to a particular community.[22] And just as Pentecost, reversing Babel, held the 'each' and the 'all' together, so the task today is to see how what is 'contextual' relates to what is 'catholic', that is, recognized by other communities and by the whole Church.

In very broad terms, we can begin to draw a continuum with four stages. At one end is *imposition*, which characterized much of the European and US missionary movements. They believed in a Christian culture which they had a duty to share, just as more conservative Anglicans today believe in an intransmutable gospel and in the Scriptures which reveal it. There are parallels here with Islam, where for example the Qur'an is to be read in Arabic rather than translated, and its moral absolutes are believed to exist whatever the cultural context.

Next along the line comes *inculturation*: how to present the message in such a way that people can hear and want to respond, and how to make the life and worship of the Church meaningful and attractive. But how far should one go? It is one thing to put a black Jesus on the cross, but what if European doctrines of the Atonement do not make much sense in African culture (or, indeed, in many Western cultures today)? It is one thing to introduce symbols and techniques from Asian religions into church worship, but at what point do they challenge the Christian identity?

An interesting example of this occurred at the 2008 Lambeth Conference, when at the opening service in Canterbury Cathedral the Bishop of Colombo concluded the sermon with a Buddhist chant in his native Sinhalese. 'Syncretism!' complained the conservative lobbyists: 'To have a Buddhist chant at an Anglican sermon does not reflect the God we believe in.'[23] The Bishop replied that the words were from St Patrick's Breastplate, to which he had done no more than Charles Wesley had done before him. Where do you draw the line? How syncretic, for example, was the Book of Common Prayer in requiring prayers for the King's majesty, or the Victorian missionaries with their 'Hymns Ancient and Modern'?

Then comes *translation*. This is not just the literal translation of the Scriptures, but even that begins a process whereby the change in words can bring a change in meaning. Indeed, the concept of 'translation' is a key one in the discussion of decolonization because it raises so many issues relating to the oppositions of inferior/superior and original/secondary, and our old question about who has the power in the process.[24] Andrew Walls calls the Incarnation 'the divine act of translation', as a result of which each age has seen a transformation of Christianity as it entered and penetrated another culture. It was this, he says, that allowed the Church to survive the fall of the Roman Empire, and which today enables the African Church to flourish away from its European roots.[25]

The classic example in mission history has been the Roman Catholic priest Vincent Donovan and his work among the Masai in Tanzania.[26] In an effort to minimize Western cultural accretions, 'he introduced what he called "the naked gospel" and then accompanied the tribesmen and women as they worked out its implications in their context and developed their own unique way of being Church'.[27] Sadly it would seem that not much of this work has survived.[28]

At the far end of this continuum, and in total contrast to imposition, comes *diversity and dialogue*. Christopher Duraisingh calls for the kind of 'decolonized imagination' which can make this possible. It means leaving what we have seen to be Western colonial thinking, such as 'the attempt to impose just one fundamental (its own), unrelated to locality or context' and 'the kind of monoculture which is actually a hegemony of power and which opposes dialogue'. He says, 'In the postcolonial vision of things, persons do not exclude each other, they simply do not co-exist nor are they assimilated into a sameness.' Rather, unity embraces diversity. He therefore wonders if the word 'postcolonial' is better replaced by words such as 'polycentric, multicultural, and dialogical'.[29]

We might try to apply some of this to the situation in which Anglicans find themselves today, taking the four elements which compose the usual processes of seeking truth: Scripture, tradition, reason and experience. The first three are directly derived from the seminal Anglican thinker Richard Hooker. Experience is an extrusion from reason and an admission that the Christian life, both individual and in the body of the Church, is always present in the process, although conservatives are more likely to see it as a modern intrusion which has caused our current disagreements.

At one end of the spectrum are those of the more conservative disposition who treat Scripture or tradition, or both, as objective realities to be passed from one generation, and one culture, to another. We have seen that this is currently represented by a convenient if somewhat strange alliance between Westerners with a conservative theology, be that Catholic or evangelical, and people from the South who come to this position from both their more traditionalist culture and from what they were taught by their founding missionaries, especially those from the more evangelical societies.

But whatever claim is made by such groups that they are staying loyal to the received faith, a process of inculturation is always happening. We have seen how US conservatives are very much part of their own consumer and capitalist society, whatever the Bible may say, and much Christianity in Asia buys into similar values through the 'prosperity gospel'. Liberals would also accuse those who support the persecution of gay and lesbian people in places like Uganda and Nigeria of being more influenced by their own culture than by the gospel.

At the other end, liberals are accused of allowing the inculturation process to give such leeway to reason and experience as to negate the prime place of Scripture and perhaps tradition. To parody the argument, if the seventeenth-century Puritans claimed to read Scripture 'without interpretation' (which is, of course, impossible, but that is what they claimed), then liberals might be accused of adopting experience 'without interpretation', and seeing Scripture and tradition only through that lens. To parody their position even further, they have gone from the Enlightenment's 'I think therefore I am' to the post-modern 'I feel therefore I think'.

Inculturation always comes to the fore in worship. What should now characterize Anglican practice? The Book of Common Prayer, at least in the revised forms undertaken by many Provinces, remains central to Anglican identity around the world. Is this centrality to continue, or to be rejected as an unwelcome leftover from the colonial attempt to impose cultural hegemony? If the Anglican traditions are to be 'translated' into more appropriate cultural forms, how far should this go?

When, for example, African churches seek such changes, should they go in the direction of their own traditional culture – the route taken by the African Independent Churches – or the more globalized culture of the US evangelists whom they see on TV? Is the increasing popularity of charismatic worship, and of Pentecostalism itself, the best or the worst of combining these two directions?

Or, to take an example from the other side, how far should the liberal church in the USA go in liturgical revision which now refers to God as Mother as frequently as it does to God as Father? Even the Baptismal Covenant – the pride of the Episcopal Church's 1979 Prayer Book – has been criticized because its commitment to 'peace, justice and respecting the dignity of every human being' precedes the sacramental act. According to one critic,

> it has lost any healthy doctrine of the righteousness of God and the sin of man. . . . [It is] a clear example of how far The Episcopal Church has become a Body deeply influenced by the European Enlightenment, where the human being not God is the center of attention in the universe, and where a major characteristic of man as an 'individual' is seen to be his freedom to choose, and his right to make agreements, even with God.[30]

One question at the root of all this is about Anglicanism itself, and how far it is the kind of 'essentialist' faith which post-modernism dismisses. It certainly appeared that way when bound up with the trappings of empire. But should it be more marked today by the *via media*, the middle way seen in the Elizabethan settlement of the English Reformation, and the kind of openness which in the last chapter was associated with an Anglican understanding of Church and mission?

Into that debate now comes the postcolonial question: which tradition, whose tradition, and what about those who now want to critique the dominant Church of England tradition from the point of view of those who were once colonized by it, and from the standpoint of the poor and neglected of today who continue to be at the receiving end of old and new imperial powers? Out of that question comes the postcolonial reading of Scripture, and all kinds of liberation theologies, including those with a strong feminist component. We have seen how the presenting issue of homosexuality has been part of all this.

It is the complaint of those Anglicans who call themselves 'traditionalists' that such theologies have 'translated' the Christian gospel to the point where they reflect the culture from which they have emerged much more than the tradition they have received, including the witness of Scripture itself. Those who make such complaints beg many questions about the nature of 'tradition', both the biblical and the Anglican, but equally – and here we come full circle – they may ask whether these newer theologies, such as the demand that the Bible should only be read 'from below', or that the right to bless same-sex partnerships is now non-negotiable, have in turn become, in parts of the Church in the USA, aspects of what we have called imposition. Has left-wing social democracy and the identification of liberation movements as movements of the Spirit of Christ become what Stephen Sykes calls a new form of Constantinianism?[31]

Faced with all these different kinds of inculturation, we are left with the question about whether the differences are now too wide, or whether what was at the other end of our spectrum – diversity and dialogue – can still be a way forward. That question, as it features in the Anglican Communion today, forms our final chapter.

7

The future of mission and Communion

————•—•—•————

Can these bones live? There are some who say that the Anglican Communion has had its day: 'it appeared by chance [and is] nothing more than a periodic conference of once like-minded individual Christians who have little now in common but a colonial past'.[1] There are some who believe that the differences between Anglicans are now so great that we should go our separate ways. Others put their hope in the proposed Covenant, but the fulfilment of that hope will depend on how the Covenant is seen to define the Communion, somewhere between an institution with fixed boundaries and a relational body which allows diversity. In this final chapter I take the experiences and arguments already described and suggest ways in which we might move forward together.

Context, power and challenge

One of the fundamental questions implicit in the kind of analyses we saw in the last chapter is: who has the power? Not just who has the power to act and change the lives of others, but who has the power to so define and determine the world that such actions are deemed either necessary or unacceptable, or to put it more simply, right or wrong? There is a real tension between the claims which Christians can make and what a writer like Foucault would call the 'diversity of reality', in which any claim to be 'normal' is a sign of power. That doesn't mean, as some ultra-liberal Christians might claim, that anything which has been 'received' from the past no longer matters, or that everyone is now free to do their own thing, but the attention to 'discourse' should at least make us aware of how people conserve their power by ignoring or excluding the other. Our colonial past should teach us that.

Christians draw significant lessons from Scripture and tradition about where power belongs and how it should be exercised, not least from Jesus himself, what he taught, and how he lived and died. We need to recognize that these lessons are often at odds with the way the world understands power. At the same time we must not be escapist. Most of us enjoy a great deal of personal power, not least in the economic sphere: we exercise choice in a way denied to many of the (rightly called) powerless in other parts of the world. And we cannot pretend that the Church is not, like every other institution, also about power relationships, especially where leadership is concerned. The question is whether in what we do, and the way we belong together, we can model something which is more Christ-like. And the challenge to do that is not in the end about being a better Church, but about showing the world how God wants it to be.

The empires of Europe and America were the context for much of the missionary era. For most of this period the churches were part of the imperial advance, and were prepared to provide justification for the national interests which took over other people's lands and often denigrated their way of life. Not surprisingly, the missionaries reflected the cultural context which had given them their own identity and direction. Some were more aware of this than others. Many helped fashion new societies enriched by education and healthcare. Such modernization helped create a new context from which local self-determination grew. Whether these new nations would have grown more healthily if traditional patterns of living had not been overthrown and resources removed, we cannot know. What we can say, not least about the trafficking of people, is that the Church was often on the side of the powers which exploited and enslaved. And they did it in the name of God.

The age of empire is not dead. Today the imperialisms are different. All kinds of powers seek to control the lives of others, and globalization provides new and powerful means to do it. This is most obvious in the economic sphere, where the global trademarks which attract consumers all around the world are only the tip of financial systems which control the distribution of resources and money through increasingly invisible and unaccountable global flows. When these systems are threatened, as they were in the financial crises of 2008, the response from politicians is not about their equity but how to protect those who benefit from them.

Imperialism is not only about economics – in the words of David Livingstone, commerce goes with civilization. In our day too those with power seek to export their value systems. As with the 'new imperialism' at the end of the nineteenth century, the aim is both to preserve the advantage of those who are making the material profit, and to bring the benefits of a supposedly superior culture. Global communication technology can make us all subject people, confronted with the Western values of (supposed) democracy and consumer choice, the more reactionary values now most closely associated with Islam, and the kind of US conservative religion that somehow manages to contain both and with which the tele-evangelists can bombard every part of the globe.

So, looking back at the history and the issues which this book has covered, I offer some final thoughts on the meaning of mission and the possibility of communion, and between them the thorny issue of human sexuality.

The Mission of God

Our starting point must always be what we believe about the gospel and the Church. Without getting over-idealistic about the early Church, clearly something dangerous happened to both gospel and Church when they became part of the Roman imperial system in the fourth century. In Luke's Gospel we read that the mission of Jesus was about 'good news for the poor', and a saving love which brought new life to those who were lost and forgotten.[2] In his second volume, the Acts of the Apostles, Luke describes a Church which grew not like an empire but by connecting with many different places where it breathed new life and created new community. Alas, the Emperor Constantine, whatever his motives, began a process which turned this gospel from an invitation into an imposition, and this Church from a fellowship (*koinonia*) into an institution.

Gospel and Church have been through many manifestations in the centuries that have followed. Anglican understandings of both have been deeply influenced by the events of the English Reformation and then the British Empire. Today, in debates where human sexuality is often the presenting issue, there are those who claim to hold a 'traditional' position, based on certain propositional truths which can never be changed. In the South this can be seen as loyalty to local tradition or more likely what the missionaries brought, while in the North it is caught up in a quite complex way with the more objectified understandings of truth which emerged at the Enlightenment. On the other side of the debate are those who have raced forwards and embraced a more 'post-modern' idea of truth, some would say based more on relationality than reality, in which everything – including the religious tradition and social institutions – is subordinated to individual choice and fulfilment.

As we've seen, recent thinking about mission has been greatly helped by the recognition that it is first and foremost what God is doing, the *Missio Dei*, rather than an activity of the Church, seeking to promote a particular product, mainly for the sake of its own self-replication. Christopher Duraisingh wonders if the *Missio Dei* is too monolithic in this pluralistic world and whether we should speak of the 'missions' (plural) of God.[3] He argues that Anglicanism is still too bound up with the European colonial project to conquer and convert the other, denigrating anything to do with multiplicity, contingency and particularity. He would rather see diversity as potentially wholesome and indeed intrinsic to the life of the Church.[4]

There is much truth in this, but also the danger of that subjectivity in which nothing has any ultimate value except to the individual who has chosen it. Perhaps the Church in Wales got the balance right when, making their response to the proposed Anglican Covenant, they said that our theology needs to be dynamic:

> It should allow for the possibility of movement and development in matters of doctrine, and should be a process which allows for an understanding of the truth as continually moving and evolving in the ongoing story of salvation and which at the same time remains faithful to the

tradition received. In its perception of the truth every generation will inevitably create new boundaries. This could be described as the dynamic praxis which directs Anglican life. It should always be mindful of the role of the Holy Spirit, the needs of the human person, the evolving nature of context and of the historical process all of which should inform the way we think about specific moral issues.[5]

Holistic mission

We saw in the discussion of the Five Marks of Mission (Chapter 4) that if the activity of God touches the whole of life, including the created order itself, then so must the witness and service of the Church. We also saw there an important question about how the first mark, 'To proclaim the Good News of God's kingdom', determines the rest. There will be a continuing debate in mission studies and in inter-faith dialogue about the role of proclamation and evangelism, although on the ground this will be determined to a large extent by the local cultural context, be it a traditional African village, an Asian city with a plurality of religions, or the kind of post-modern city which we increasingly see in the UK.

An essential part of this mission is the changing of unjust structures and the struggle for economic justice. This is not a return to the social gospel which characterized much of US Episcopalianism during the last century. I trust that this book has been very clear that these things are not the whole of mission, and has been critical of those, including some Christian development agencies, who have reduced the gospel to poverty reduction and human rights. Such matters are nevertheless an indispensable part of what we are called to do, a part without which the rest lacks credibility and integrity.

Where do Anglican churches stand? In the North both conservatives and liberals are very much part of the prevailing economic systems and beneficiaries of them. How can we be more active in envisioning and seeking to enact different systems where the poor of the world can have a greater say and a larger share? In some parts of the South poverty is so endemic that even the churches take it for granted or feel powerless to change it. How might more of them engage in development and stand with the poor, identify more with their people than the local elites, and avoid being led astray by Western agendas?

Such struggles are not only about political and economic change but also present a deeper gospel challenge to the way in which modern culture sees people and their society. One of the effects of globalization has been the 'commodification' of people and the reduction of values to mere consumerism. Commenting on the 2009 Reith Lectures, in which the US economist Michael Sandel called for a remoralization of politics, the British religious commentator Madeleine Bunting says: 'we must correct a generation of abdication to the market of all measures of value. Most political questions are at their core moral or spiritual . . . They are about our vision of the common good; bring religion and other value systems back into the public sphere for a civic renewal.'[6]

This brings us to the safeguarding of Creation, a late addition to the Five Marks of Mission. Much of the damage to the planet, now perhaps irreparable, has been due to the 'commodification of creation', arising from the loss of previous understandings of purpose and gift. The churches have been relatively slow to see the urgency of this issue, hence the late addition. Its inclusion may show how our understanding of God's mission is a matter of continuing discovery. International debates on climate change disclose where power lies in our world, and those who will suffer most in places like Bangladesh and the Pacific have the least power of all.

Environmental degradation also relates to those deeper questions about the post-modern world. To quote Madeleine Bunting again:

> the only grand narrative on offer is so terrifying – of a world rapidly running out of the natural resources required to sustain extravagant lifestyles and burgeoning population – that it disables rather than empowers us to achieve political change. . . . Every other modern narrative – communism, socialism, even those that were destructive, such as neoliberalism and fascism – laid claim to a version of the kingdom of God, a better world that would nurture a better human being. They were all narratives of redemption and salvation. All that we have now is apocalypse, and it is paralysing. How then can we build hope?[7]

Partnership in mission

I now turn to more practical matters of how the different parts of the Anglican Communion support each other in God's mission, but again the deeper issues are present. How do we avoid the old imperialisms whereby one part, the part with the power, defines what the mission is and how the other parts should do it? That applies to those with the material power, to both Western liberals and conservatives who reinvent colonialism when the strings on their money are attached to their own particular theology. It also applies to those who may now be seen to have the 'spiritual' power, the growing churches of the South, where some leaders refuse support – at the expense of their church members, who may need it most – from those with whom they disagree, and others claim the right to tell those in the 'decadent West' how they should do their mission.

Our patterns of support should not recreate the kind of dependencies in which those who are able to provide material support determine the mission priorities of the recipients. We have seen how 'partnership' can become a slippery word when the Western donor-culture requires not just information and accountability – which can be signs of a mature partner relationship – but projects, reports and even visits which are more to do with meeting the whims of the donor than the needs of the local church. Americans have never left such attitudes behind, and there are many signs of British Christians returning to what is essentially a form of colonialism. It is, again, a manifestation of those consumerist values which the gospel should be challenging.

That leads me to speak again about the role of mission agencies, and clearly what I say will seem like special pleading from someone who runs one! Whatever their role in our imperial past, the agencies today can play a vital role in Communion-wide mission. They are not restricted to the one small part of the Communion which a companion link may have chosen. They do not carve up the gospel between development work and evangelism. They take the Church seriously as both part of God's mission and an essential agent of it. At their best they are the means for the different parts of the Communion, geographically and theologically, to meet and plan together.

The actual relationship of these agencies to the Church remains interesting. As we have seen, SPG always saw itself as the 'handmaid of the Church', with its work under the direction of the local bishop, while CMS was more suspicious of those bishops who were not of its own persuasion. That latter relationship can still be found today in certain situations where the mission agency maintains a presence somewhat apart from the local church, remaining accountable instead either to local people who share the agency's views or to supporters in another part of the world. In the USA the missionary society is still in theory the Episcopal Church itself, but in fact the Church has also spawned a number of separate agencies, and even 'official' church activity is now performed more by the dioceses than through the national offices. Those mission agencies which have retained some independence may be able to offer more of a critical edge to the local church, whether that's a call for more evangelism or for more social engagement, but the risk of 'new colonialisms', of imposing their own agendas, remains great, especially when they bring external resources.

Human sexuality

I have suggested that this is often only the presenting issue in areas of disagreement, but nevertheless it is so prominent in the Communion's conflicts, and so disruptive of our common mission, that we must deal with it here. Again, questions about who is telling the story come into play, not just in particular contexts such as that of a church (perhaps in Asia) trying to survive in a primarily Islamic country or a church (perhaps in North America) seeking to engage with a secularized culture, but also in matters of who is defining whom. A prime part of the Communion's 'listening process', and now of the Continuing Indaba, has been to let gay and lesbian people speak for themselves.

Although there are no easy answers, perhaps we can identify the challenges which those who have taken up particular positions on homosexuality need to face. First, those in the South need to look more closely at their own context: their traditional culture and the patriarchy which was often an essential part of it; what powers were at work in the changed thinking the missionaries brought, and more recently that brought by Western conservatives seeking allies abroad; why some see it differently – for example in South Africa where, as in the US experience, it can be a justice issue like racial equality; and how other parts of Resolution I.10 from the 1998 Lambeth Conference denouncing homophobia go against any church support for anti-gay legislation, as exemplified recently in Nigeria and Uganda.

Second, those in the North who have embraced the inclusivity agenda also have work to do. Much of the argument up to now has been concerned with achieving justice for those whose natural sexual identity has been either rejected or refused expression. In the UK, organizations like Inclusive Church see statements such as Archbishop Rowan Williams's 'Covenant, Communion and the Anglican Future' as going back on his past support for those in stable, permanent and loving same-sex relationships.[8] The Episcopal Church is increasingly recognizing, and in places solemnizing, same-sex partnerships as equal to marriage, although probably accepting that many will be as fractured and serial as their heterosexual equivalents in contemporary America. Other developments in North America suggest something more: same-sex relationships, especially between women, are less about a given orientation and more about the rejection of male-orientated power-dominated relationships. Those who support these developments claim that they encourage relation-ships which mirror the kind of love which God has for us. Their critics say that they are replacing any traditional Christian understand-ing of marriage with what is essentially a lifestyle choice.

Finally, those in the North who have lobbied against change also have much answering to do. These include groups like Anglican Mainstream and now the Anglican Church of North America. The power of technology and the power of money have both been at work in taking advantage of the genuine concerns of people in the South and trying to persuade them to give the issue a much higher priority than they might otherwise have thought necessary. The whole Communion needs to honour the integrity of those bishops who refuse such advances and who, whatever their misgivings, came to the 2008 Lambeth Conference as a sign of their commitment to a wider vision.

Leadership

Much power in the Communion rests with its bishops, but this is not to say that only bishops should exercise leadership in the Church. Indeed, the role of the laity impinges heavily on current disputes, from the very different polity of the Episcopal Church in which bishops do not have the sole power to respond (even if they so wished) to directives from the rest of the Communion, to the belief that the future of the Communion should be in the hands of a much more representative and synodical body, perhaps an extension of the Anglican Consultative Council, in which lay people can exercise more authority.

Nevertheless, bishops play a large part in the ordering of the Anglican Church, and how they use that power has always determined its mission. From St Paul onwards Christian leaders have pressed and even bullied those who would not toe their line, even when speaking of a Christ-like surrendering of power! It's said that a more monarchical form of episcopacy emerged in the early Church in order to defend doctrines from heresy. In the 1940s Gerald Broomfield, General Secretary of UMCA, pressed the Bishops of Zanzibar and Nyasaland to involve clergy and laity in their diocesan constitutions with the words, 'There has been some talk recently about the dictatorships of Bishops.'[9]

Views differ as to whether the more authoritarian style of episcopacy found in many African churches arises from their traditional culture and the role of a tribal chief, or from what the first Western bishops imported from the Church of England. Trevor Mwamba, Bishop of Botswana, says:

> The totem of the Manja tribe in the Central Africa Republic is the rabbit because it has 'large ears'. The Manja stress listening as the most important characteristic of the chief. . . . The problem in the Anglican Communion is that the bishops have 'short ears'. Which means we are hard of hearing, all deafened by the noise of our respective agendas. The great tragedy speaking as an African bishop is that having 'short ears' makes some of our Primates in Africa act like ecclesiastical Mugabes. . . . The spirit of African Anglicans is not inclined to schism but reconciliation.[10]

91

Similarly, the Tanzanian bishop Simon Chiwanga, a former chairman of the Anglican Consultative Council, attributes any abuse of power to the 'dependence mentality' created by colonialism. He wants to rethink episcopacy from the more traditional African values of running an extended family, with the bishop as 'mhuduma' – the servant, not the chief – within the 'ujamaa' – the community of the Church. In this model, he says, the bishop enables interpretation of the gospel, builds up the members and inspires hope. We move from sovereign to mutual, from episcopocentric to polycentric, so enabling 'the apostolicity of the whole church'.[11]

All of which could take us back to the beginning, for when Augustine arrived in Canterbury in 597 he was carrying Gregory the Great's 'Book of Pastoral Rule', in which the Pope had written: 'All who are superiors should not regard in themselves the power of their rank, but the equality of their nature; and they should find their joy not in ruling over men but in helping them.' Perhaps he was being reminded of what the first St Augustine said in a sermon: 'For you I am the bishop, with you I am a Christian.'[12] That leads me to my final two words: *diakonia* and *koinonia*.

Diakonia[13]

The exercise of power has been a constant theme running through this book, from the politics of England (especially through the Reformation period) to the imperial ambitions of the missionary era, and in what I have called the 'new colonialisms' which seek to direct the cultures, economies, and indeed churches of our own day. When the author Philip Pullman is accused of pursuing an anti-Christian agenda in novels like his 'Dark Materials' trilogy, he responds that he is not attacking Christianity itself so much as the constraints and dangers of dogmatism and the use of religion to oppress. 'How easy it is', says the Ghanaian theologian John Pobee, 'for the Church and the faith to be accommodated to political ideology, particularly the power ideology.'[14]

In marked contrast is the Christian concept of *diakonia* (sometimes translated 'service'), rooted in the words of Jesus: 'I am among you as one who serves.'[15] It begins, as St Paul wrote to the Philippians, with the Incarnation when Jesus 'emptied himself, taking the form of a slave, being born in human likeness',[16] and finds its apogee when Jesus washes the disciples' feet and challenges them to do the same: 'If I, your Lord and Teacher, have washed your feet, you also ought to wash one another's feet. For I have set you an example, that you also should do as I have done to you.'[17]

If such surrendering of power, this *kenosis*, seems a tall order, there's an important reminder in Kirsteen Kim's book on mission, written through a focus on the Holy Spirit, that we empty ourselves in order to be filled with the power of the Spirit to carry on Christ's work. More than that, she says that it is here that we 'encounter the underside of the incarnation, the movement of the Holy Spirit in the world which subverts earthly power structures and challenges hegemony'.[18]

What might this mean in practice? We saw that colonialism was based on a 'binary' understanding of reality, one thing against another, and ordered in a hierarchy. It led to a 'winner takes all' mentality. All sides in the Communion's current conflicts might learn from Michael Ramsey's warning against claiming to have a superior knowledge of the truth: 'It has been the role of Anglicanism to criticize other Christian traditions that claim to know too much . . . The credibility of Anglicanism lies not in its own virtues or successes but in . . . Jesus, crucified and risen, who through his Church still converts sinners and creates saints.'[19]

So *diakonia* points to a different understanding of power. Martyn Percy describes it as 'this profoundly kenotic activity [where] a new power is gained, yet it is one that does not and cannot dominate. Rather, resurrection power transforms, by inviting participation into the being a communion of God', and he contrasts this with 'models of ministry based on the exercise of power which compels, punishes and bullies, [and which] actually distort and pervert the Gospel and eclipse the life and presence of God'.[20]

Miroslav Volf, who grew up in the violence of Croatia and is now a US Episcopalian, has written about the search for reconciliation which rejects the usual claim to moral purity and the usual call for retribution. The cure, he believes, is for Christians to reclaim the faith's original content – grace, forgiveness, reconciliation, justice – and live as agents of peace. The cross, he says, is 'the narrative of the love of the divine Trinity turned toward a sinful world'. He offers yet another way in which the Trinity can lead us to relationships which are not based on power: 'Just as Father, Son, and Holy Spirit have distinct identities yet live in unity, people who become new creations in Christ retain their identities – and make space for others.'[21]

Koinonia

The Christian concept of *koinonia* (sometimes translated 'fellowship') connects all those understandings of communion which we saw underlying the *Missio Dei*: from the very nature of the Holy Trinity to the life of the Church and God's will for all humankind. Bruce Kaye calls it the 'priority to participate in the divine life through Christ and to do that for the sake of the mission which is God's in the world'.[22] True *koinonia* cannot be separated from a genuine *diakonia* within its members, but my aim in this final section is to look at some of the more corporate issues of being in (Anglican) Communion today.

The Roman Catholic missiologist Robert Schreiter might be addressing the Anglican Communion rather than criticizing his own church when he calls for a 'new catholicity' which can only be achieved by intense intercultural exchange and communication in an attitude of generosity and respect towards other Christians from whom we may differ.[23]

We have already noted Christopher Duraisingh's work on the catholic and the contextual, in which he recognizes that while the gospel is for all times and all places it must nevertheless be embodied in a particular culture – all theology is contextual. Nevertheless it can never be identified with that culture because it transcends all cultures. 'What is needed is a rejection of both the postmodern radical relativism and its notion of incommensurability of cultures, as well as the Enlightenment claims for all-encompassing and ahistorical meta-framework and universals.'[24]

He asks more specifically whether Anglicanism continues to reflect the European colonial project to conquer and convert the other and the strange, or whether like the gospel it can be more stranger-centred, with a love for 'the other'. Can we affirm both diversity of traditions and the possibility of community across differences? Can we develop a *koinonia* which confronts both the 'totalism' and the 'tribalism' with which Martin Marty characterizes the modern world?[25] This is both a theological issue, with deep implications for how far different approaches and understandings of the gospel live together in one communion, and a deeply practical one when dealing with what kind of communion we are and what structures we need. Both are to do with power.

There will always be questions about where the Anglican tradition should find itself in this very different kind of world. It was shaped by English nationalism: does its vaunted *via media*, originally the middle way between Catholicism and Puritanism, reek of political compromise or provide a starting point for the embracing of new diversity? It grew in association with British imperialism: Terry Brown, until recently a bishop in Melanesia, wants to distance himself from that 'hegemony model' and embrace instead the kind of 'loving hybridity' which he found in the way that the Solomon Islanders have dealt with incoming influences.[26] Bruce Kaye asks whether we can now put aside the old (imperial) authority which declares truth by dogmatic assertion or coercive power. He proposes other ways forward which also arise from the Anglican tradition: confidence ('Persuasive Resonance'), community ('Interdependent Diversity') and engagement ('Respectful Visionaries').[27]

So we need to find structures which will help us to hold and develop this *koinonia*. Anglicanism is not a Church (like the Roman Catholic one), nor is it a confession (like the Lutherans), but it is more than a federation (like the worldwide Baptists). It is a communion of churches, in which, says Martyn Percy, there is 'dispersed authority' and 'directional pluralism'.[28] For some, both African and American, that allows unilateral action, while others call for more centralized decision-making.

Is an Anglican Covenant the answer? This proposal is not, says Archbishop Rowan Williams, 'an effort to create . . . a centralised decision-making executive but a "community of communities" that can manage to sustain a mutually nourishing and mutually critical life, with all consenting to certain protocols of decision-making together'.[29]

But I share the fears of others that it could become a quick-fix solution designed to preserve the status quo, to provide procedural methods for conflict resolution, rather than a commitment which leads to transformation and reconciliation.[30]

I believe that in the end *koinonia* must be eucharistic rather than structural. We see it when people meet and share around a common table because they have been called by God and they recognize each other to be 'in Christ'. The peace that is given does not come from common history or chosen friendship; it is the Peace of Christ. Our communion, our Anglican Communion, our communion together in the body and blood of Christ, is God's invitation and God's gift. It is the bread we must break, not each other, because Christ has already been broken for us. If our *koinonia* cannot embrace difference, allow change, contain challenge, what witness are we to the world? For in the end our communion together is not for the sake of the Church, but so that we may be a living sign of God's reconciled human community.

For me, the most moving part of the 2008 Lambeth Conference was the daily Eucharist, and how, when it came to the Lord's Prayer, we were encouraged to say it each in our own language. A subdued hubbub ensued, as we prayed the same prayer but out of many different cultures and conditions.[31] It had much in common with Pentecost, where what happened was not that the apostles spoke the same language, but that somehow despite all their different languages they were able to listen and hear each other. Surely, when we speak of 'unity in diversity' and 'being in communion', it is this which we seek and for which we must continue to struggle.

Notes

1 The expansion of the Church of England

1 Sebastian Kim and Kirsteen Kim, *Christianity as a World Religion*, London: Continuum, 2008.

2 Noel Davies and Martin Conway, *SCM Core Reader on Christianity in the 20th Century*, London: SCM Press, 2008.

3 John O'Farrell, *An Utterly Impartial History of Britain*, London: Black Swan, 2007.

4 Eamon Duffy, *The Stripping of the Altars: Traditional Religion in England c.1400–c.1580*, New Haven, CT: Yale University Press, 1992.

5 It was also used to remove land rights from native peoples in the United States, and was repudiated by the TEC General Convention in 2009. See <http://www.indiancountrytoday.com/national/southwest/51572857. html>.

6 W. M. Jacob, *The Making of the Anglican Church Worldwide*, London: SPCK, 1997.

7 Daniel O'Connor (ed.), *Three Centuries of Mission: The United Society for the Propagation of the Gospel 1701–2000*, London: Continuum, 2000.

8 C. F. Pascoe, *Two Hundred Years of the S.P.G.: an historical account of the Society for the Propagation of the Gospel in Foreign Parts, 1701–1900*, London: SPG, 1901.

9 Jacob, *Making of the Anglican Church*.

10 Jacob, *Making of the Anglican Church*.

11 Jeffrey Cox, *The British Missionary Enterprise Since 1700*, London: Routledge, 2008.

12 Noel Titus, 'Concurrence without compliance: SPG and the Barbadian plantations', in O'Connor (ed.), *Three Centuries of Mission*.

13 Vincent T. Harlow, *The Founding of the Second British Empire*, London: Longmans, 1964.

14 See the article on Henry Martyn in Brother Tristram SSF, *Exciting Holiness*, London: SCM Canterbury Press, 2007.

15 Andrew Porter, 'An Overview, 1700–1914', in Norman Etherington (ed.), *Missions and Empire*, Oxford: Oxford University Press, 2005.

16 Sydney Smith, 'Indian Missions', *Edinburgh Review*, April 1808.
17 George Watson, 'Joseph Butler', in Hugh Sykes Davies and George Watson (eds), *The English Mind: Studies in the English Moralists*, Cambridge: Cambridge University Press, 1964.
18 Matthew 28.18–20.
19 Bishop Shipley, *A Sermon Preached Before the Incorporated Society for the Propagation of the Gospel in Foreign Parts*, 1773.
20 Jacob, *Making of the Anglican Church*.
21 Andrew Porter, *Religion Versus Empire? British Protestant Missionaries and Overseas Expansion, 1700–1914*, Manchester: Manchester University Press, 2004.
22 John S. Pobee, *AD 2000 and After: The Future of God's Mission in Africa*, Ghana: Asempa Publications, 1991.
23 A. B. Lloyd, Preface to *In Dwarf Land and Cannibal Country*, London: T. Fisher Unwin, 1907.
24 H. H. Montgomery, *The Life and Letters of George Alfred Lefroy*, London: Longmans, Green and Co., 1920.
25 John H. Darch, *Missionary Imperialists? Missionaries, Government and the Growth of the British Empire in the Tropics 1860–1885*, Milton Keynes: Paternoster, 2008.
26 Kevin Ward and Brian Stanley (eds), *The Church Mission Society and World Christianity 1799–1999*, Grand Rapids, MI: Eerdmans, 2000.
27 Lamin Sanneh, 'The CMS and the African Transformation: Samuel Ajayi Crowther and the Opening of Nigeria', in Ward and Stanley (eds), *Church Mission Society*.
28 Darch, *Missionary Imperialists?*.
29 Dana L. Robert, *Converting Colonialism: Visions and Realities in Mission History 1706–1914*, Grand Rapids, MI: Eerdmans, 2008.
30 Steven Maughan, 'Imperial Christianity – Bishop Montgomery and the Foreign Missions of the C of E, 1895–1915', in Andrew Porter (ed.), *The Imperial Horizons of British Protestant Missions, 1880–1914*, Grand Rapids, MI: Eerdmans, 2003.
31 H. H. Montgomery, *Foreign Missions*, London: Longmans, Green and Co., 1902.
32 Cox, *British Missionary Enterprise*.
33 Brian Stanley, *The Bible and the Flag*, Leicester: Apollos, 1990.
34 Stephen Neill, *Colonialism and Christian Missions*, London: Lutterworth, 1966.
35 Darch, *Missionary Imperialists?*.

36 Norman Etherington, 'Missions and Empire', in W. Roger Lewis (ed.), *Historiography*, vol. 5 of *The Oxford History of the British Empire*, Oxford: Oxford University Press, 1999.

37 Lamin Sanneh, *Encountering the West: Christianity and the Global Cultural Process*, Maryknoll, NY: Orbis, 1993.

2 The emergence of the Anglican Communion

1 Ian T. Douglas, *Fling Out the Banner: The National Church Ideal and the Foreign Mission of the Episcopal Church*, New York: Church Hymnal Corporation, 1996. Much of this section draws heavily from Bishop Douglas's work when at the Episcopal Divinity School, Cambridge, MA.

2 Douglas, *Fling Out the Banner*.

3 W. M. Jacob, *The Making of the Anglican Church Worldwide*, London: SPCK, 1997.

4 Colin Podmore, *Aspects of Anglican Identity*, London: Church House Publishing, 2005.

5 Resolution 11 of the Lambeth Conference, 1888.

6 J. R. Wright, 'Anglicanism, Ecclesia Anglicana and Anglican: An Essay in Terminology', in S. W. Sykes and J. E. Booty (eds), *The Study of Anglicanism*, London: SPCK; Minneapolis: Fortress Press, 1988.

7 Ruth Rouse and Stephen Neill (eds), *A History of the Ecumenical Movement, Vol. 1, 1917–1948*, Geneva: WCC Publications, 2002.

8 *World Missionary Conference 1910: The History and Records of the Conference*, Edinburgh and London: Oliphant, Anderson & Ferrier, 1910.

9 <http://www.lambethconference.org/resolutions/1908/>.

10 'Colonialism is Doomed', speech to the 19th General Assembly of the United Nations in New York City by Cuban representative Che Guevara on 11 December 1964.

11 Quoted in John S. Pobee, 'The Anglican Church in Ghana and the SPG', in Daniel O'Connor (ed.), *Three Centuries of Mission: The United Society for the Propagation of the Gospel 1701–2000*, London: Continuum, 2000.

12 Stephen Neill, *Christian Missions*, Harmondsworth: Penguin, 1964.

13 Adrian Hastings, *History of African Christianity 1950–1975*, Cambridge: Cambridge University Press, 1979.

14 Elliott Kendall, *The End of an Era – Africa and the Missions*, London: SPCK, 1978.

15 *Report of the Proceedings of the Anglican Congress 1963*, Toronto: Anglican Book Centre, 1963.

16 Douglas, *Fling Out the Banner*.

17 Duncan Reid, *Journal of Anglican Studies*, June 2005.

18 <http://www.anglicancommunion.org>.

19 <http://www.anglicancommunion.org/acns/news.cfm/2009/11/27/ACNS4671>.

20 TEAC Consultation, Singapore, May 2007: <http://www.anglicancommunion.org/ministry/theological/signposts/english.cfm>.

21 <http://www.lambethconference.org/resolutions/1930/>.

22 <http://www.anglicancommunion.org/commission/process/index.cfm>.

23 The full text of the Covenant can be found at <http://www.anglicancommunion.org/commission/covenant/final/text.cfm>.

24 Rowan Williams, 'Communion, Covenant and our Anglican Future'. See <http://www.archbishopofcanterbury.org/2502>.

25 Section 5:20, *The Virginia Report: The Report of the Inter-Anglican Theological and Doctrinal Commission*, London: Anglican Consultative Council, 1997.

26 Henry Orombi, Archbishop of Uganda, on Anglican TV (based in Connecticut, USA), 4 August 2009.

27 Fourth Anglican Global South to South Encounter: <http://www.globalsouthanglican.org/index.php/archives/category/statements>.

28 Bruce Kaye, *Conflict and the Practice of the Christian Faith*, Eugene, OR: Cascade Books, 2009.

29 Bruce Kaye, *Reinventing Anglicanism: A Vision of Confidence, Community and Engagement in Anglican Christianity*, Adelaide, South Australia: Openbook Publishers, 2003.

30 <http://www.anglicancommunion.org/commission/covenant/docs/18_wales.pdf>.

31 <http://www.inclusivechurch2.net/uploads/media/Peter_Selby_-_when_the_word_on_the_street_is_resist.pdf>.

32 John Barton, 'Covenant in the Bible and Today', in Mark D. Chapman (ed.), *The Anglican Covenant: Unity and Diversity in the Anglican Communion*, London: Mowbray, 2008.

3 The Anglican Communion today

1 Alan Stephenson, *Anglicanism and the Lambeth Conferences*, London: Camelot Press, 1978.

2 The resolutions from Lambeth Conferences since 1867 can be found at <http://www.lambethconference.org/resolutions/index.cfm>.

3 *The Virginia Report: The Report of the Inter-Anglican Theological and Doctrinal Commission*, London: Anglican Consultative Council, 1997.

4 *The Windsor Report*, report of the Lambeth Commission on Communion, London: Anglican Communion Office, 2004. <http://www.anglicancom munion.org/windsor2004/index.cfm>

5 Lorraine Cavanagh, *By One Spirit: Reconciliation and Renewal in Anglican Life*, Oxford: Peter Lang, 2009.

6 Karen Armstrong, *The Battle for God: Fundamentalism in Judaism, Christianity and Islam*, London: HarperCollins, 2000.

7 Article VI, Thirty-Nine Articles of Religion, Book of Common Prayer.

8 Lambeth Quadrilateral, as accepted by the Lambeth Conference, 1888.

9 Bishop Michael Nazir-Ali, *Daily Telegraph* interview, 29 August 2009.

10 Press Conference at the London launch of FOCA, June 2008.

11 Kwok Pui-lan in Ian T. Douglas and Kwok Pui-lan (eds), *Beyond Colonial Anglicanism: The Anglican Communion in the 21st Century*, New York: Church Publishing, 2001.

12 Quoted in Cavanagh, *By One Spirit*.

13 Ephraim Radner, *Anglican Theological Review*, Fall 2000.

14 Brian J. Grieves, *No Outcasts: The Public Witness of Edmond L. Browning*, Cincinnati, OH: Forward Movement Publications, 1997.

15 From Bishop John Shelby Spong's website <www.johnshelbyspong.com>, October 2010.

16 Michael Doe, *Seeking the Truth in Love*, London: Darton, Longman & Todd, 2000.

17 Michael Doe, 'From Colonialism to Communion', *Journal of Anglican Studies* Vol. 7, November 2009.

18 Miranda K. Hassett, *Anglican Communion in Crisis*, Princeton, NJ: Princeton University Press, 2007.

19 Kevin Ward, 'Same-sex Relationships in Africa and the Debate on Homosexuality in East African Anglicanism', *Anglican Theological Review*, Winter 2002.

20 Hassett, *Anglican Communion in Crisis*.

21 *Observer*, 12 October 2003: <http://www.guardian.co.uk/world/2003/oct/12/religion.anglicanism>.

22 See 'Following the Money' at <http://www.edow.org/follow/>.

23 *Globalizing the Culture Wars*, Political Research Associates, 2009: <http://www.publiceye.org/ark/africa-report/pdf/africa-full-report.pdf>.

24 Gayle Harris, *Washington Post*, 9 August 2008.

25 <http://www.dioceseofvermont.org/DioConvention%202005/Resolutions Approved05.html>.

26 Harris, *Washington Post*, 9 August 2008.

27 Pitt Lecture at the Berkeley Divinity School, Yale University, October 2009.

4 The mission of God and the Anglican tradition

1 David Bosch, *Transforming Mission*, Maryknoll, NY: Orbis, 1991.
2 Jürgen Moltmann, *The Church in the Power of the Spirit: A Contribution to Messianic Ecclesiology*, London: SCM Press, 1977.
3 USPG Anglicans in World Mission, *Our Theological Basis and Ways of Working*, 2008.
4 Bosch, *Transforming Mission*.
5 John V. Taylor, *The Uncancelled Mandate*, London: Church House Publishing, 1998.
6 'Bonds of Affection', ACC-6, and 'Mission in a Broken World', ACC-8, London: Anglican Consultative Council, 1984 and 1990.
7 'Bonds of Affection'.
8 *Communion in Mission*, Report of IASCOM (Inter-Anglican Commission on Mission and Evangelism), London: Anglican Communion Office, 2006.
9 Timothy Yates, 'David Bosch: South African Context, Universal Missiology – Ecclesiology in the Merging Missionary Paradigm', in *International Bulletin of Missionary Research*, April 2009.
10 Titus Presler, *Horizons of Mission*, Cambridge, MA: Cowley Publications, 2001.
11 *Communion in Mission*.
12 The Virginia Report, in the *Official Report of the Lambeth Conference 1998*, London: Anglican Communion Office, 1999: <http://www.lambethconference.org/1998/documents/report-1.pdf>.
13 Bruce Kaye, *An Introduction to World Anglicanism*, Cambridge: Cambridge University Press, 2008.
14 <http://www.rethinkingmission.org.uk/pdfs/bpdoejun08.pdf>; <http://www.anglicancommunion.org/ministry/theological/signposts/english.cfm>.
15 Lambeth Conference 1998: Resolution II.1.
16 'The Anglican Way: Signposts on a Common Journey', Report from the Singapore Consultation of the Theological Education in the Anglican Communion (TEAC) Working Party of the Anglican Primates, 2007.
17 *Lambeth Indaba: Capturing Conversations and Reflections from the Lambeth Conference 2008 – Equipping Bishops for Mission and Strengthening Anglican Identity*, London: Anglican Consultative Council, 2008.
18 *The Virginia Report: The Report of the Inter-Anglican Theological and Doctrinal Commission*, London: Anglican Consultative Council, 1997.
19 *Communion in Mission*.
20 *Virginia Report*.

21 'The Anglican Way'.
22 'The Anglican Way'.
23 Michael Ramsey, *The Gospel and the Catholic Church*, London: Longmans, 1936.
24 Lambeth Conference 1998: Resolution II.6.
25 *Communion in Mission*.
26 'An Anglican Covenant', St Andrews Draft Text, 2008.
27 E.g. Stephen Sykes, John Booty and Jonathan Knight (eds), *The Study of Anglicanism*, London: SPCK, 1998.
28 E.g. Paul Avis, *The Identity of Anglicanism*, London: T & T Clark, 1998.
29 Alastair Redfern, *Being Anglican*, London: Darton, Longman & Todd, 2001.
30 Ian T. Douglas, 'The Exigency of Times and Occasions: Power & Identity in the Anglican Communion Today', in Ian T. Douglas and Kwok Pui-lan (eds), *Beyond Colonial Anglicanism: The Anglican Communion in the 21st Century*, New York: Church Publishing, 2001.
31 Kaye, *Introduction to World Anglicanism*.
32 Lorraine Cavanagh, *By One Spirit: Reconciliation and Renewal in Anglican Life*, Oxford: Peter Lang, 2009.

5 The Church in mission today

1 Colossians 3.11.
2 *The Virginia Report: The Report of the Inter-Anglican Theological and Doctrinal Commission*, London: Anglican Consultative Council, 1997.
3 *Virginia Report*.
4 <http://www.anglicancommunion.org/communion/acc/meetings/acc2/index.cfm>.
5 <http://www.csitirunelveli.org/ministry/ministry_ims.htm>.
6 Michael Jaffarian, 'Are There More Non-Western Missionaries than Western Missionaries?', *International Bulletin of Missionary Research*, July 2004.
7 Report of the San Antonio Conference, CWME 1989, Geneva: WCC Publications, 1990.
8 <http://www.anglicancommunion.org/ministry/mission/commissions/missio/d_doc.cfm#s17>.
9 Ian Douglas, 'Authority, Unity and Mission in the Windsor Report', *Anglican Theological Review*, Fall 2005.
10 See, for example, John Stuart, 'Overseas Mission, Voluntary Service and Aid to Africa: Max Warren, the CMS and Kenya', *Journal of Imperial and Commonwealth History*, September 2008.

11 'The Development of Peoples', Papal encyclical, March 1967.

12 <http://www.lausanne.org/covenant>.

13 Johannes Christiaan Hoekendijk, *The Church Inside Out (Adventures in Faith)*, Geneva: WCC, 1966.

6 Globalization and the post-colonial Church

1 Michel Foucault, *The Archaeology of Knowledge* [1969], London: Routledge, 1972.

2 Jacques Derrida, *Of Grammatology* (corrected edition), trans. Gayatri Chakravorty Spivak, Baltimore and London: Johns Hopkins University Press, 1998.

3 Richard Rohr, in Richard Tiplady (ed.), *Postmission: World Mission by a Postmodern Generation*, Carlisle: Paternoster, 2002.

4 John S. Pobee, *Exploring Afro-Christology*, New York: Peter Lang, 1992.

5 Agbonkhianmeghe Orobator, *Theology Brewed in an African Pot*, Maryknoll, NY: Orbis, 2008.

6 Karen Armstrong, *The Battle for God: Fundamentalism in Judaism, Christianity and Islam*, London: HarperCollins, 2000.

7 Martin Marty, 'From the Centripetal to the Centrifugal', *Theology Today*, April 1994.

8 John Reader, *Reconstructing Practical Theology: The Impact of Globalization*, Aldershot: Ashgate, 2008.

9 Martyn Percy, *Power and the Church: Ecclesiology in an Age of Transition*, London: Cassell, 1998.

10 Miranda K. Hassett, *Anglican Communion in Crisis*, Princeton, NJ: Princeton University Press, 2007.

11 Vatican press release, 4 October 2009.

12 Philip Jenkins, *The Next Christendom: The coming of global Christianity*, Oxford: Oxford University Press, 2002.

13 Roger Bowen, 'Genocide in Rwanda 1994 – an Anglican Perspective', in C. Rittner, J. K. Roth and W. Whitworth (eds), *Genocide in Rwanda: Complicity in the Church?*, St Paul, MN: Paragon House, 2004.

14 Hassett, *Anglican Communion in Crisis*.

15 Jenkins, *Next Christendom*.

16 Helen Gilbert and Joanne Tompkins, *Post-Colonial Drama: Theory, practice, politics*, London: Routledge, 1996.

17 Robert J. C. Young, *Postcolonialism: A Very Short Introduction*, Oxford: Oxford University Press, 2003.

18 Edward W. Said, *Orientalism*, New York: Pantheon, 1978.

19 Frantz Fanon, *The Wretched of the Earth* [1961], Harmondsworth: Penguin, 2001.

20 Ian T. Douglas and Kwok Pui-lan (eds), *Beyond Colonial Anglicanism: The Anglican Communion in the 21st Century*, New York: Church Publishing, 2001.

21 Andrew F. Walls, *The Missionary Movement in Christian History: Studies in the Transmission of Faith*, Maryknoll, NY: Orbis, 1996.

22 Christopher Duraisingh, 'Contextual and Catholic: Conditions for Cross-Cultural Hermeneutics', in *Anglican Theological Review*, Fall 2000.

23 <http://www.guardian.co.uk/world/2008/jul/21/anglicanism.religion>.

24 E.g. Susan Bassnett and Harish Trivedi (eds), *Post-Colonial Translation: Theory and Practice*, London: Routledge, 1999.

25 Walls, *Missionary Movement in Christian History*.

26 Vincent J. Donovan, *Christianity Rediscovered: An Epistle to the Masai*, Maryknoll, NY: Orbis, new edition 2003.

27 Kirsteen Kim, *Joining In with the Spirit: Connecting World Church and Local Mission*, Peterborough: Epworth, 2010.

28 'What happened next? Vincent Donovan, thirty-five years on', *International Bulletin of Missionary Research*, April 2009.

29 Christopher Duraisingh, in Douglas and Pui-lan, *Beyond Colonial Anglicanism*.

30 The late Revd Dr Peter Toon, President of the Prayer Book Society, USA, at <www.virtueonline.org>, 28 December 2006.

31 Stephen Sykes, *Power and Christian Theology*, London: Continuum, 2006.

7 The Future of mission and Communion

 1 Edward Norman, *Anglican Difficulties: A New Syllabus of Errors*, London: Morehouse, 2004.

 2 Michael Doe, *Today! The Mission of Jesus in the Gospel of Luke*, London: USPG Publications, 2008.

 3 Christopher Duraisingh, 'Encountering Difference in a Plural World', in Ian T. Douglas (ed.), *Waging Reconciliation: God's Mission in a Time of Globalization and Crisis*, New York: Church Publishing, 2002.

 4 Christopher Duraisingh, 'Contextual and Catholic: Conditions for Cross-Cultural Hermeneutics', *Anglican Theological Review*, Fall 2000.

 5 <http://www.anglicancommunion.org/commission/covenant/docs/18_wales.pdf>.

 6 Madeleine Bunting, <guardian.co.uk>, 28 June 2009.

 7 Bunting, <guardian.co.uk>, 28 June 2009.

 8 <http://www.inclusivechurch2.net/On-the-Archbishop-s-Reflections-0467221>.

9 Andrew Porter, 'The Universities' Mission to Central Africa: Anglo-Catholicism and the Twentieth-Century Colonial Encounter', in Brian Stanley (ed.), *Missions, Nationalism and the End of Empire*, Grand Rapids, MI: Eerdmans, 2003.

10 Trevor Mwamba, Bishop of Botswana, Modern Churchpeoples' Union Conference, 2008.

11 Simon Chiwanga, 'Beyond the Monarch/Chief: Reconsidering Episcopacy in Africa', in Ian T. Douglas and Kwok Pui-lan (eds), *Beyond Colonial Anglicanism: The Anglican Communion in the 21st Century*, New York: Church Publishing, 2001.

12 St Augustine of Hippo, Sermon 340.

13 I am indebted to Bishop Idris Jones, former Primus of the Episcopal Church of Scotland, and Dr Jenny Plane-Te Paa from the College of St John the Evangelist, Auckland, New Zealand, for their contributions to the 2009 USPG National Conference which prompted this section.

14 John S. Pobee, *AD 2000 and After: The Future of God's Mission in Africa*, Ghana: Asempa Publications, 1991.

15 Luke 22.27.

16 Philippians 2.7.

17 John 13.14–15.

18 Kirsteen Kim, *Joining in with the Spirit: Connecting World Church and Local Mission*, Peterborough: Epworth, 2010.

19 Michael Ramsey, *The Anglican Spirit*, Cambridge, MA: Cowley Publications, 1991; New York: Church Publishing, 2004 (reprint).

20 Martyn Percy, *Power and the Church: Ecclesiology in an Age of Transition*, London: Cassell, 1998.

21 Miroslav Volf, *Exclusion and Embrace: Theological Exploration of Identity, Otherness and Reconciliation*, Nashville, TN: Abingdon Press, 1996.

22 Bruce Kaye, *Reinventing Anglicanism: A Vision of Confidence, Community and Engagement in Anglican Christianity*, Adelaide, South Australia: Openbook Publishers, 2003.

23 Robert J. Schreiter, *The New Catholicity: Theology between the Global and the Local*, Maryknoll, NY: Orbis, 1997.

24 Duraisingh, 'Contextual and Catholic'.

25 Martin Marty, *The One and the Many: America's Struggle for the Common Good*, Cambridge, MA: Harvard University Press, 1997.

26 Terry Brown, 'Abandoning the Hegemonic Model', *Journal of Anglican Studies*, June 2006.

27 Kaye, *Reinventing Anglicanism*.

28 Percy, *Power and the Church*.

29 Rowan Williams, address at the Willebrands Symposium in Rome, November 2009.

30 Lorraine Cavanagh, *By One Spirit: Reconciliation and Renewal in Anglican Life*, Oxford: Peter Lang, 2009.

31 Michael Doe, 'From Colonialism To Communion: Lambeth 2008 In Retrospect', *Journal of Anglican Studies*, Winter 2009.

Index